RADICAL DECADENCE

Excess in contemporary feminist textiles and craft

JULIA SKELLY

Bloomsbury Academic
An imprint of Bloomsbury Publishing Plc

BLOOMSBURY
LONDON · OXFORD · NEW YORK · NEW DELHI · SYDNEY

Bloomsbury Academic

An imprint of Bloomsbury Publishing Plc

50 Bedford Square	1385 Broadway
London	New York
WC1B 3DP	NY 10018
UK	USA

www.bloomsbury.com

BLOOMSBURY and the Diana logo are trademarks of Bloomsbury Publishing Plc

First published 2017

British Library Cataloguing-in-Publication Data
A catalogue record for this book is available from the British Library.

ISBN: HB: 978-1-4725-6941-7
PB: 978-1-4725-6940-0
ePDF: 978-1-4725-6942-4
ePub: 978-1-4725-6943-1

Library of Congress Cataloging-in-Publication Data
Names: Skelly, Julia, author.
Title: Radical decadence: excess in contemporary feminist textiles and craft/Julia Skelly.
Description: New York: Bloomsbury Academic, 2017. | Includes bibliographical references.
Identifiers: LCCN 2016041060 (print) | LCCN 2016043094 (ebook) |
ISBN 9781472569400 (paperback) | ISBN 9781472569417 (hardback) |
ISBN 9781472569424 (ePDF) | ISBN 9781472569431 (ePUB)
Subjects: LCSH: Feminism and art. | Women artists. | Art and craft debate. |
Excess (Philosophy) | BISAC: SOCIAL SCIENCE/Feminism & Feminist Theory. |
DESIGN/Textile & Costume.
Classification: LCC N72.F45 S59 2017 (print) | LCC N72.F45 (ebook) | DDC 704/.042–dc23
LC record available at https://lccn.loc.gov/2016041060

Cover design by Catherine Wood
Cover image © ChristinaK / Getty Images

Typeset by Deanta Global Publishing Services, Chennai, India
Printed and bound in India

RADICAL DECADENCE

"My dear fellow, as if I cared!"

—Oscar Wilde, *The Picture of Dorian Gray* (1891)

CONTENTS

LIST OF ILLUSTRATIONS

Plates

Figures

Introduction

Chapter 4

ACKNOWLEDGMENTS

I am grateful to the staff at the National Art Library, London; the Ruthin Craft Centre; the Wellcome Library; the Textile Museum of Canada, Toronto; and Concordia University's library, Montreal. As ever, I'm grateful to Scott Jacobs at the William Andrews Clark Memorial Library, UCLA. Dr. Janice Helland has been a continuous source of inspiration and support since I first took her class on feminism and art at Queen's University in 2003. I am fortunate to have several friends and colleagues who see the humorous side of academia. I would like to acknowledge especially Christina Smylitopoulos and Steven Stowell. I am grateful for research funding from the Friends of the Archives, Centre for Addiction and Mental Health, Toronto. At Bloomsbury, I have had the pleasure of working on this book with Hannah Crump, Ariadne Godwin, Agnes Upshall, and Pari Thomson. My anonymous readers' comments, critiques, and suggestions were immensely helpful. Finally, I want to extend my sincere appreciation to the artists who granted permission to include their work in *Radical Decadence*.

INTRODUCTION: DECADENCE, FEMINISM, AND "EXCESS"

Craft and feminist art histories

As feminist craft historian and artist Janis Jefferies has observed, "The taste for the decorative was pathologised as feminine, as embellishment, as style, as frivolous, as excessive and was therefore constantly repressed within the rhetorical devices of Modernism." She adds that "detail and fabric were viewed as decorative extras and excluded from the rigid confines of the regularly ordered space in the pictorial plane. Once released, detail and pattern become excessively magnified and erupted, even exceeding the borders which once tried to contain them."[1] This passage beautifully describes the ways that textiles, detail, and pattern have been framed as excessive in the history of Western art. Jefferies's words are also useful for considering how women, often deemed "excessive" because of their bodies and behaviors, have pushed against—"exceeded"— the gendered norms that have tried to contain them.

Radical Decadence is a book about feminism, excess, and pleasure, art made out of fiber and porcelain and canvas and paint and rhinestones. I discuss cupcakes, cocaine, velvet, socks, dirty linens, pornography, and hangovers, among other things. This is the stuff of everyday life, and I will be approaching these subjects from the perspective of a feminist art historian who has undertaken research on late-nineteenth-century discourses of addiction and decadence, as well as research on contemporary feminist art. This book is ultimately an attempt to bring those various fields in dialogue, employing what I call "radical decadence" as a theoretical apparatus for considering the works of several different artists from several different countries. *Radical Decadence* was initially conceptualized as a book about pleasure and contemporary feminist textiles and craft, which is to say, a book about pleasure and contemporary feminist art that is made out of materials that have traditionally been associated with so-called "craft," namely textiles and porcelain, despite the fact that, as Svetlana Alpers reminds us, painting was long described and thought of as a "craft."[2]

This is to enter the still thorny terrain of the art/craft hierarchy, according to which "art" (gendered as masculine and produced by primarily male artists) has been privileged in Western art history over "craft," which at a certain point in history became gendered as feminine, "women's work," that lacked the ingenuity and genius attributed to paintings made by men. This is well-trodden ground and Rozsika Parker has discussed it much better than I ever could. As she notes early on in *The Subversive Stitch: Embroidery and the Making of the Feminine* (1984):

> The development of an ideology of femininity coincided historically with the emergence of a clearly defined separation of art and craft. This division emerged in the Renaissance at the time when embroidery was increasingly becoming the province of women amateurs, working for the home without pay. Still later the split between art and craft was reflected in the changes in art education from craft-based workshops to academies at precisely the time—the eighteenth century—when an ideology of femininity as natural to women was evolving.[3]

In *Old Mistresses: Women, Art and Ideology* (1981), co-written by Parker with feminist art historian Griselda Pollock, the authors critique early feminist art historians for merely inserting women artists into (masculine) art history—identified as the "recuperation model"—rather than dismantling the discipline itself, including the art/craft hierarchy. Parker and Pollock examine the strategy in early feminist art history celebrating needlework as important in the history of women's creative production, but they argue that this feminist methodology does not go far enough in deconstructing the very discipline of art history:

> While women can justifiably take pride in these areas, asserting their value in the face of male prejudice does not displace the hierarchy of values in art history. By simply celebrating a separate heritage we risk losing sight of one of the most important aspects of the history of women and art, the intersection in the eighteenth and nineteenth centuries of the development of an ideology of femininity, that is, a definition of women and their role, with the emergence of a clearly defined separation of art and craft.[4]

That critique was written over twenty years ago, and a great deal of scholarship on women artists, feminism, and craft has since been written. While I will not endeavor to write an in-depth literature review of this scholarship here, it goes without saying that the work of scholars such as Parker, Pollock, Linda Nochlin, Lynda Nead, Rosemary Betterton, Carol Duncan, Janice Helland, Kristina Huneault, and Janis Jefferies, among many others, has paved the way for the present study.[5]

Feminist artists in the 1970s also set out to disrupt the art/craft hierarchy. Between 1974 and 1979, Judy Chicago, in collaboration with hundreds of seamstresses, produced *The Dinner Party* (Plate 1), which comprises 39 table settings (including an embroidered runner, chalice, and painted ceramic plate) along a large three-sided table, each plate "representing a woman (actual or mythological) of historical significance."[6] Chicago has said that she conceived of the work as a Last Supper for women, because at Jesus's last supper all of the women would have been in the kitchen. *The Dinner Party* is an example of the kind of recuperative project that Parker and Pollock critiqued, and the work, though popular with the public, was often dismissed in the art press as feminist propaganda. Chicago deliberately included both ceramics and textiles in the work to point to the kind of objects that had been left out of traditional art history. In addition, some of the place settings were for women artists who had been left out of survey texts and survey courses. Janis Jefferies has remarked that this kind of "potentially radical yet problematic promotion of women's 'traditional' arts in textiles enabled not only a distancing from an aesthetics of the 'purely' visual but also provided a strategy for mobilising textiles as a weapon of resistance against an inculcated 'feminine' ideal."[7]

It is worth underscoring the fact that Jefferies uses the phrase "potentially radical" to describe feminist artists' use of textiles. I argue in this book that feminist artists' use of craft materials, such as fiber, is a radical artistic and ideological act, but because of ongoing stigmas related not only to craft materials and practices, but also to some of the subject matter addressed by artists including Orly Cogan, Tracey Emin, and Mickalene Thomas (drug use, abortion, and black female sexuality, respectively), the works discussed in *Radical Decadence* will be perceived as radical by some viewers and problematic by others. Alexandra Kokoli has discussed the historical ambivalence toward women's craft, which Parker illuminates in *The Subversive Stitch*, noting that at times this ambivalence "gets lost within a discourse that celebrates women's craft as inherently Revolutionary,"[8] particularly when there is uncritical nostalgia for the domestic or for a "simpler time." Significantly, none of the works in *Radical Decadence* celebrate domesticity, or are even "simply" about domesticity, despite their use of domestic textiles. Nava Lubelski's *Clumsy* (Plate 5), a stained tablecloth, is radical in the sense that she is capturing in thread a moment of domestic failure, and by extension, a moment of failure as, or of, a woman.

It is no coincidence that these artists are using craft materials (fiber, ceramic, rhinestones) to engage with taboo subject matter. Indeed, I want to propose that the ostensible "excessiveness" of craft materials—positioned as superfluous, decorative, and *unnecessary* in traditional and modernist art histories—make them the perfect materials for the representation of ostensible excesses in the lived experiences of women. Thus materiality is crucial to the understanding of *radical decadence*.[9] Subject matter and materials are inextricably woven together. Subjects include women's drug use, women's alcohol consumption, and women's self-fashioning through clothes, cosmetics, and luxury goods. Might we describe these works, then, as "narrative" works? If so, what stories are they telling?[10] African American artist Faith Ringgold has been producing story quilts for many years, illuminating the intersections between black female histories and craft materials.[11] What would happen if Cogan's subjects (women consuming cupcakes and cocaine) were painted in oils or acrylics on canvas? Would they have the same impact, or would they be dismissed as kitsch? Mickalene Thomas's paintings *are* painted in acrylic, yet critics have often avoided calling her works "paintings," because they also incorporate rhinestones, to some viewers' dismay, as I discuss in Chapter 2. Thus these artists' choice of materials is crucial for the feminist, critical work that they are doing. Jefferies has commented upon "the characteristic flexibility and softness of textile works," and "the multiplicity of forms of a creative language that is unique to fibre and qualities of the decorative" open space for craft materials to be used in innovative, subversive, and radical ways.[12]

Judy Chicago cofounded the Feminist Art Program at California State University in 1971, expanding the program later that year with artist Miriam Shapiro and moving it to California Institute for the Arts, where it ran until 1975.[13] Despite her significant contributions as a feminist artist, because of her "essentialist" vision of a feminine aesthetic, for example, her use of "core imagery," later feminist artists distanced themselves from her work and ideas. More recent feminist artists, however, such as Canadian Allyson Mitchell, have brought Chicago's oeuvre to the attention of a younger generation. As Mitchell wrote in the catalogue for *When Women Rule the World: Judy Chicago in Thread* (2009), "It is difficult to discuss the history of feminist art without acknowledging the contributions of Judy Chicago. Best known for her epic (and controversial) project, *The Dinner Party*, Chicago has dedicated her 40-year career to redressing the profound lack of female artists and feminine iconography canonized in the history of Western art."[14] Mitchell observes that *The Dinner Party* "is particularly notable for its attempt to elevate traditionally feminine or domestic craft (needlework, china painting) to the realm of high art, lending significance to the everyday practices of ordinary women."[15]

It is important that I establish early on the significance of feminist art history for my methodology, because I will be using the term "decadence" quite often in this book, and decadence has usually been associated with men and male artists. Therefore, in a book concerned with both decadence and feminism, I want to demonstrate that these concepts are not mutually exclusive. Rather, transformed into *radical decadence*, the concept of decadence can be employed to critically examine artworks that speak to "excess" and the exceeding, or refusing, of gendered norms and ideologies, including those related to what art "is" and what it "should" be made out of.

Excess, of course, is relative and culturally contingent. I return frequently to Mary Russo's concept of the "female grotesque" in this book, because Russo demonstrates how the "excessive" woman is recognized as excessive only in relation to gendered norms. She also reminds us that there are always risks in living excessively.[16] I propose that *radical decadence* is a deliberate form of excess, or of exceeding ideological (as well as spatial) boundaries. I take decadence to mean in this context a concern with pleasure—whether in terms of consumption, production, or spectatorship—as well as with luxury, artifice, and refusal, among other things. Edward Lucie-Smith observes that late-nineteenth-century "decadence . . . can often be defined in terms of refusals," which "calls attention to the generally negative aspects of the Symbolist emotional climate. Symbolism was a way of saying 'no' to a number of things which were contemporary with itself."[17] From a feminist perspective, this definition of decadence is useful in that it illuminates the many refusals that radically decadent artists are enacting, including the refusal of art-historical ideologies, gendered norms, feminine roles (such as wife and mother), and shaming discourses related to the consumption of food, alcohol, and drugs.[18] "Excess" can be a deliberate aesthetic, or it can be a derogatory term that is projected onto certain women for certain behaviors. Like "decadence," the term "excess" has often been used to shame and/or control that which threatens the social order.

By using the phrase *radical decadence,* I am of course invoking the radical feminist politics of the 1960s and 1970s,[19] as well as "radical art history," which is dedicated to intervening in traditional, masculinist discourses related to art, representation, and gender.[20] According to Jayne Wark, "The idea that art could be political was in itself a radical concept in the late 1960s and into the 1970s because the art world was still dominated by the belief that the purpose of art was either to transcend or to provide an alternative to the crude exigencies of social struggle and political strife."[21] Wark focuses her analysis on feminist performance art in North America, arguing that it "played a decisive role in negotiating a new relationship between art and politics."[22] One of the premises of *Radical Decadence* is that the artists' choice to work with materials historically associated with craft is in itself a radical, political move because of the traditional denigration of craft made by women. These materials, then, namely ceramics and textiles, are symbolically loaded materials used for radical, feminist purposes. As Alexandra Kokoli has written, "The very nature of feminist intervention is dynamic and expansive: it either brings on a radical reshuffling of social and semiotic systems on the whole, or it is ineffective."[23] In the same edited volume, Griselda Pollock observes that "feminist work is transgressive of existing institutions and structures in which it nonetheless has to intervene, and to which it should make a radical difference."[24] *Radical decadence*, then, as a feminist approach to both art and life, is predicated upon a desire to engender change and make a difference.

Decadence and women

It is not insignificant that in the late nineteenth century there were intermingled fears about decadence and degeneration, as articulated by Max Nordau, among others, as well as anxieties about the New Woman. As Linda Dowling has shown, the New Woman and the male aesthete, rather than enemies or opposites, were in fact allies who caused anxieties related to gender, sex, and the propagation of the (white European) race. Dowling observes: "To most late Victorians the decadent was new and the New Woman decadent. The origins, tendencies, even the appearance of the New Woman and the decadent—as portrayed in the popular press and periodicals—confirmed their near, their unhealthily near relationship. Both inspired reactions ranging from hilarity to disgust and outrage, and both raised as well profound fears for the future of sex, class, and race."[25] She adds: "Critics of the fin de siècle avant-garde thus understood a truth that has now grown obscure: in a cultural context of radical anxiety, the decadent and the New Woman were twin apostles of social apocalypse."[26] While not, perhaps, portending the apocalypse, the artists discussed in *Radical Decadence*, in pushing against gendered and sexed boundaries, as did the (male) decadent and the New Woman in the late nineteenth century, demand a critical analysis that does not stop at the (superficial) "decadent" elements in their work—namely, rich materials and subjects that include drug consumption, sexual behavior, and "excessive" eating—but rather one that examines these decadent elements for the very boundaries they are transgressing, whether they be within the discipline of art history or within categories of normative femininity.

The late nineteenth century was also the historical moment when the *femme fatale* was a central figure in both literature and art produced by men as a way of coping with fears about women who had become discontent with their lot in life as angels in the house.[27] Perhaps it goes without saying, but in books about Symbolist and/or decadent art (these terms are often used interchangeably, or at least in relation to one another), the works are invariably by men depicting threatening, devouring women such as sphinxes and vampires.[28] The *fin-de-siècle* decadent was regarded as male, albeit an effeminate male, related to the male aesthete; indeed, the figures of the "decadent" and the "aesthete" have often been construed as overlapping or interchangeable.[29] Kimberly Wahl has shown that women were very much part of the Aesthetic movement that Oscar Wilde, among others, championed, and she discusses the slippage from aestheticism to the more morally dubious concept of decadence:

> Early in its development, consensus of the importance of health and beauty in dress resulted in the cooperation of Aesthetic dressers and dress reformers intent on social change. Later, as Aestheticism became progressively associated with decadence, artistic excess, and moral and physical forms of corruption, the more politicized dress reform circles began to disassociate themselves from Aesthetic dressing as a viable form of social criticism and practice.[30]

Decadence was gendered masculine, but it was usually conceived of in relation to a problematic, worrisome, "non-normative" masculinity. Arthur Symons, author of "The Decadent Movement in Literature" (1893), identified excess, self-absorption, chaos, and effeminacy as characteristics of the decadent male.[31] George Mosse has noted that decadence was linked with both addiction and a lack of virility: "Nervousness and hysteria lay at the centre of Decadence, whether symbolized by that lack of restraint, which, so it was said, had led to the fall of the Roman Empire, or to weakness and sterility brought about by 'physical and moral poison' such as alcoholism, the use of opium or debilitating disease."[32] This "lack of restraint," associated with drugs and alcohol, among other things, was perceived as the decadence that preceded the decay and decline of great empires: first Rome, then the British Empire, as Lynda Nead has discussed in *Victorian Babylon*.[33] Although there were certainly rampant anxieties about women's drug consumption—particularly the consumption of morphine—decadence was, and continued to be, discussed primarily in relation to men and male artists.[34]

   The vast majority of scholarship on decadence, both in the nineteenth century and more recently, has focused on male writers and artists such as Charles Baudelaire and Oscar Wilde. Richard Gilman's rather grumpy analysis in *Decadence: The Strange Life of an Epithet* (1975) is limited to male writers. He quotes the poet Paul Verlaine, for instance, as stating: "I like the word 'decadent'. . . . All shimmering with purple and gold . . . it throws out the brilliance of flames and the gleam of precious stones."[35] Gilman was ultimately concerned with the fact that in the twentieth century, people were using the term "decadent" in ways that, according to Gilman, were inaccurate, etymologically speaking. I feel fairly confident that he would have frowned upon my use of the term in this book. Early in his text Gilman remarks:

> Words take on life from a particular environment and time, but certain of them live on beyond their proper course and duration. Most archaic words have obeyed inexorable linguistic laws; the life has gone out of them and they remain merely as historical artifacts, coinage from an earlier realm of the mind. But there are words that are not so docile, so tractable. They hang on, simulating existence, lending themselves for use with an alacrity that ought to make us suspicious. Certain words of a moral or

behavioral kind, judgmental words, continue to insinuate themselves into contexts where they injure meaning and bring about confusion, since they carry with them a *previousness*, something once true, something, that is to say, once applicable. There are words in use now that are no longer applicable.[36]

The term "decadence" was often used pejoratively at the end of the nineteenth century, and it was frequently a coded term for nonheterosexuality, but usually in relation to same-sex desire between men. Elaine Showalter remarks that "decadence is a notoriously difficult term to define. In one sense, it was the pejorative label applied by the bourgeoisie to everything that seemed unnatural, artificial, and perverse, from Art Nouveau to homosexuality, a sickness with symptoms associated with cultural degeneration and decay."[37]

There were those in the late nineteenth and early twentieth centuries who—despite, or perhaps because of—the negative connotations of the term "decadence," actively embraced the concept as a strategy for self-fashioning. Martin Green discusses how young men in Britain after the First World War reappropriated Wildean decadence as a way of rejecting their fathers' generation.[38] Like Gilman, Green ignores women's possible relationships with, and uses of, decadence. Linda Dowling has effectively described this tendency:

> The tradition in studies of the Victorian fin de siècle has been to identify such figures as Oscar Wilde and Aubrey Beardsley with a tendency then and now known as Decadence, and in Decadence to see a cultural episode with sensational or lurid overtones. This is the controlling impulse, for instance, behind Rupert Croft-Cooke's portrayal of Wilde in *Feasting with Panthers*, a treatment that may well linger as the last reminder of the older view. There is Wilde pursuing his insatiable way from one male prostitute to the next, Wilde reclining on a couch talking of poetry and art and ancient Rome, pressing candied cherries from his own lips to those of his young companion, Wilde leaving tipsily for the night with his chosen calamite. . . . And like so many established views, this one contains its measure of truth; Croft-Cooke's source for all this is the court records of Wilde's trial for homosexual practices in 1895, a proceeding that remains emblematic not least because Decadence, too, was on trial.[39]

Significantly, several feminist scholars have critically discussed decadence in visual culture and literature by both men and women.[40] In *The Gender of Modernity* (1995), Rita Felski comments: "Positioned on the margins of respectable society, yet graphically embodying its structuring logic of commodity aesthetics, the prostitute and the actress fascinated nineteenth-century cultural critics preoccupied with the decadent and artificial nature of modern life."[41] Later in her book, Felski notes that "the familiar and still prevalent cliché of the insatiable female shopper epitomizes the close associations between economic and erotic excess in dominant images of femininity."[42]

Felski's statement is relevant for the present study in that several of the artists discussed in *Radical Decadence* are concerned with intersecting excesses related to consumption and the female body: Orly Cogan represents women, often naked save for socks, consuming cupcakes and cocaine (Plate 2); Canadian artist Shelley Miller produces luxury handbags made out of cake, which she sometimes displays on pedestals and subsequently has friends decimate (that is, eat), which Miller captures in photographs (Figure 1.3). With *Clumsy* (Plate 5), Nava Lubelski has produced a tablecloth with a large red stain that functions as a trace of an invisible (female) wine drinker, while British artist Tracey Emin, who was often linked with alcohol and cigarettes during the 1990s, has produced works that speak to the woman who consumes vodka and who has been known, on occasion, to have sex. Ghada Amer's paintings that incorporate both paint and thread often portray women in the throes of sexual pleasure (Plate 11). I argue in Chapter 3 ("Bad Women?") that these works are "excessive" not only because of their content, but also because of Amer's self-reflexive use of thread (as impasto) to exceed the ideological and gendered boundaries historically ascribed to painting.

Readers will note that in addition to decadent artist Aubrey Beardsley (Figures 0.1–0.7), the work of another male artist, Shane Waltener, is examined in *Radical Decadence*. Even if Waltener does not identify as a feminist artist, his performative cake workshop *Sweet Nothings* (2005) is an important counterpoint to consider in relation to Orly Cogan's works that represent isolated young women consuming cupcakes and cocaine. Likewise, I discuss at least one female artist who has explicitly rejected the term feminist. Tracey Emin has publicly distanced herself from feminism, as I discuss in Chapter 3. Nonetheless, I examine both Waltener's and Emin's work through the feminist lens of radical decadence in order to illuminate how the two artists are engaging with gendered ideologies related to excess, consumption, and pleasure.

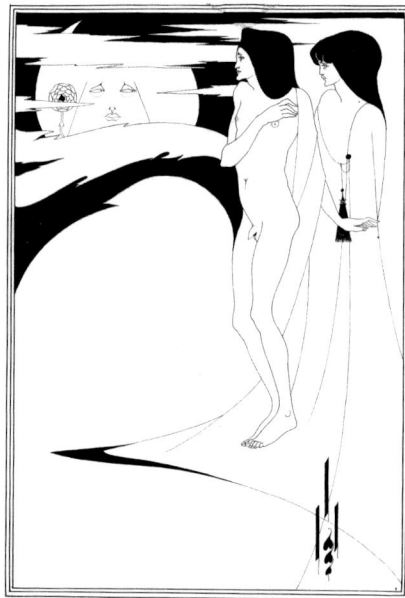

Figure 0.1 Aubrey Beardsley, *The Woman in the Moon*, 1893. Black ink and graphite on white wove paper. 23 × 16.5 cm (9 1/16 × 6 ½ in.) Harvard Art Museums/Fogg Museum, Bequest of Grenville L. Winthrop, 1943.643. Photo: Imaging Department © President and Fellows of Harvard College.

Figure 0.2 Aubrey Beardsley, *The Peacock Skirt*, for *Salomé*, 1893. Black ink and graphite on white wove paper. 23 × 16.8 cm (9 1/16 × 6 5/8 in.). Harvard Art Museums/Fogg Museum, Bequest of Grenville L. Winthrop, 1943.649. Photo: Imaging Department © President and Fellows of Harvard College.

Figure 0.3 Aubrey Beardsley, *John and Salome*, 1893. Black ink and graphite on white wove paper. 23.3 × 16.4 cm (9 3/16 × 6 7/16 in.) Harvard Art Museums/Fogg Museum, Bequest of Grenville L. Winthrop, 1943.651. Photo: Imaging Department © President and Fellows of Harvard College.

Figure 0.4 Aubrey Beardsley, *The Eyes of Herod*, for *Salomé*, 1893. Black ink and graphite on white wove paper. 22.9 × 16.9 cm (9 × 6 5/8 in.). Harvard Art Museums/Fogg Museum, Bequest of Grenville L. Winthrop, 1943.631. Photo: Imaging Department © President and Fellows of Harvard College.

Figure 0.5 Aubrey Beardsley, *The Stomach Dance*, for *Salomé*, 1893. Black ink and graphite with corrections in white gouache on white wove paper. 22.6 × 16.6 cm (8 7/8 × 6 9/16 in.). Harvard Art Museums/Fogg Museum, Bequest of Grenville L. Winthrop, 1943.634. Photo: Imaging Department © President and Fellows of Harvard College.

Figure 0.6 Aubrey Beardsley, *The Dancer's Reward*, for *Salomé*, 1893. Black ink and graphite on white wove paper. 23 × 16.5 cm (9 1/16 × 6 1/2 in.). Harvard Art Museums/Fogg Museum, Bequest of Grenville L. Winthrop, 1943.652. Photo: Imaging Department © President and Fellows of Harvard College.

Figure 0.7 Aubrey Beardsley, *The Burial of Salome*, 1893. Black ink and graphite on white wove paper. 16.4 × 17.4 cm (6 7/16 × 6 7/8 in.) Harvard Art Museums/Fogg Museum, Bequest of Grenville L. Winthrop, 1943.642. Photo: Imaging Department © President and Fellows of Harvard College.

Other works discussed in *Radical Decadence* are less obviously about ostensible excesses related to consumption but are read in terms of the pleasures of (feminist) spectatorship and the pleasures of looking at (and wanting to touch) certain materials: the sheen of black porcelain in Mickalene Thomas's sculptures (Figure 2.4), the sparkle of rhinestones in her paintings (Plates 7 and 8), the luminous shine of Shary Boyle's white monstrous women (Plate 9), and the lure of velvet and lace in works by Rozanne Hawksley (Plates 13–16). These works are read as "decadent" and "excessive" not only because of their materials, but also because of what they portray or imply: women (viewers) seeking after and experiencing pleasure.

Cherchez la femme

The female body is absent in many of the works discussed in *Radical Decadence*: Emin's *My Bed*, Lubelski's *Clumsy*, Rozanne Hawksley's gloves. Conversely, the female body is represented in most (though not all) of Orly Cogan's works, Mickalene Thomas's works, and Shary Boyle's porcelain sculptures. Rather than representing a human female, Canadian artist Jessica Sallay-Carrington's fat rabbit is an allegory of body positivity (Figure 0.8). Sallay-Carrington has created an animal stand-in for the woman who luxuriates in her body, enthroned on a velvet cushion. Mary Russo discusses the fat woman as corporeal excess, taking up more space then she "should." She remarks that "fat women in the United States particularly, are repositories of shame and

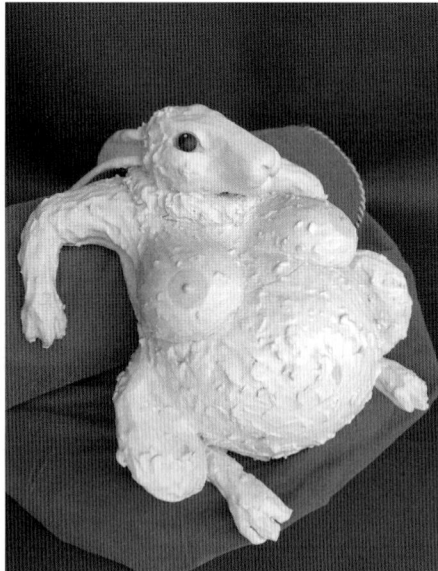

Figure 0.8 Jessica Sallay-Carrington, *Fat Rabbit and All Her Glory*, 2012. Porcelain and velvet cushion, 20" × 9" × 20". Collection of the artist.

repressed desire."[43] Sallay-Carrington's fat rabbit refuses shaming discourses, and it is no coincidence that she uses porcelain and velvet in this work.

As many feminist scholars have shown, textiles are deeply symbolic, resonant materials because of the historical relationships between women and cloth that have been both oppressive and liberating.[44] These histories and relationships are woven throughout *Radical Decadence* in discussions of craft and addiction discourse (Chapter 1), pleasure (Chapter 2), and failed or "bad" women (Chapter 3). Ceramics too are symbolically loaded for women artists. Cheryl Buckley notes that "women have been actively involved in the production and consumption of ceramics in most societies," but like many women working in other media, female producers of ceramics were long written out of art history.[45] Significantly, Buckley concludes that "the relationships between ceramics and feminism are fruitful avenues for further investigation, not least because of the longevity, pervasiveness and complexity of women's engagement with this area of cultural activity."[46] With this in mind, Shary Boyle's and Mickalene Thomas's ceramic works are discussed in Chapter 2.

The absence of the female body in some, though not all, of the works examined in *Radical Decadence* is significant in the context of feminist art, because following the period of feminist body art of the 1960s and 1970s, some feminist artists and art historians became wary of representing the female body, which had already been represented to death in Western art by male artists, as well as in pornography and popular culture. Peggy Phelan commented on this hypervisibility of the female body: "If representational visibility equals power, then almost-naked young white women should be running Western culture."[47] Janis Jefferies observes that, "while a model of critical practice had been crucial in establishing the visibility of feminist discourses and practices, it also became increasingly narrowly employed to promote a prescriptive and proscriptive conception of 'proper' feminist art practice, which seemed to admonish sensual or visual pleasure."[48] More recent feminist artists have returned to the female body as a site of both excess and resistance, and artists discussed in this book who represent the female body—whether white or black, in porcelain, thread, or paint—are doing so against a complex history of the represented female body in visual culture. All of the works, however, push against what might be considered "proper" craft or textile art, and that is why they are included in this book: these works are excessive in the sense that they exceed what has traditionally been perceived as acceptable in both textiles and women's art; they are decadent in terms of their materials and their subjects; and they are radical in the sense that they are contributing to dialogues about gender, pleasure, societal norms, and art in new and transgressive ways intended to engender change, whether for individual viewers or in the larger art world.

Decadence, culture, and feminism

In *Reading in Detail: Aesthetics and the Feminine* (1987), Naomi Schor writes: "Of all the arguments enlisted against the detail, none was to receive more attention in the mid-nineteenth century than the ancient association of details and decadence, which runs in an unbroken continuity from the critique of realism to the critique of modernism."[49] Her work on the detail and "bad objects" is particularly relevant for a study on (feminist) textiles and craft, because historically, and still to a certain extent in certain circles, craft objects were deemed "bad objects." According to Schor, the identification of "bad objects" can be "traced to any number of causes: their aesthetic inappropriateness, their subversive possibilities, their pettiness. Pleasure, fear, boredom, and power are all forces that might render a specific critical topos either a bad or a good object."[50] Her consideration of "bad objects" is ultimately a consideration of "hierarchies of value,"[51] one of which is the art/craft hierarchy.

Schor argues that the detail discloses "its participation in a larger semantic network, bounded on one side by the *ornamental*, with its traditional connotations of effeminacy and decadence, and on the other, by the *everyday*, whose 'prosiness' is rooted in the domestic sphere of social life presided over by women."[52] Ornament, of course, has been read, like craft, as in opposition to art, in that it is *in excess*, and it has been gendered as feminine and associated with primitive cultures, for example in Adolf Loos's essay "Ornament and Crime" (1908).[53] Feminist art historians Bridget Elliott and Janice Helland have written: "Implying excess, supplementarity and play, ornament was also subject to changes in fashion, all of which threatened the historical transcendence and universal truth claims that many leading modernists wanted their art to embody."[54] Even more significantly for *Radical Decadence* as a whole and Chapter 3 in particular, Schor observes: "To deliberately make an object choice branded as bad is risky business at worst and at best a means to go beyond certain impasses, to read at an angle, to be an intellectual bad girl."[55] She is concerned here with a theorization of female fetishism, appropriating the term despite its masculinist and misogynistic histories. This is an example of "paleonymy," which she defines as "the use of an old word for a new concept."[56] In the following chapters, I propose to undertake a similar project with the concept of "decadence."

A third feminist literary scholar's work is relevant to the following discussions, because she introduces visual culture into her analysis of late-nineteenth-century decadent literature.[57] In *Art and Anger: Reading Like a Woman* (1988), Jane Marcus argues that "Wilde's life and work were important to the notions of sexual freedom championed by Bloomsbury. He also made it clear that aestheticism could be seen as morally and politically radical against the background of earnest Victorian philistinism."[58] In 1891, before he stood trial for gross indecency, Wilde wrote a play entitled *Salomé*, in French, which was illustrated by Aubrey Beardsley in 1893 (Figures 0.1–0.7). According to Marcus, Wilde disliked Beardsley's drawings. He told artist Charles Ricketts: "They are all too Japanese, while my play is Byzantine. My Herod is like the Herod of Gustave Moreau — wrapped in jewels and sorrows. My Salome is a mystic, the Sister of Salammbö, a Sainte Thérèse who worships the moon; dear Aubrey's designs are like the naughty scribbles a precocious schoolboy makes on the margins of his copybook."[59] Marcus notes that "Salome was the icon of the ideology of the decadents. She fascinated many artists, most notably Moreau and Beardsley, but also many lesser-known painters."[60] Salome was also one of the iconic *femmes fatales* of the late nineteenth century, who was used as a cipher, or even as a coping strategy, for the anxieties revolving around women's increased demand for political equality and sexual freedom embodied by the figures of the suffragette and the New Woman, respectively.[61] Marcus proposes that Wilde's Salome can be interpreted as a New Woman, or even as a suffragette with a rock in her hand, but she argues that

> Wilde's Salome bears very little resemblance to the Salome of Beardsley's drawings, Moreau's paintings, or the description of them in Huysmans's *Au rebours*. Late nineteenth-century painting, from the Pre-Raphaelites to the decadents, mannerists, and symbolists, had presented either the virgin or the whore as its image of woman. There are some interesting variations, of course, but in either guise, she is usually associated with death. The revival of all the mythological, historical, and royal figures of perverse and powerful women from Sappho to the sphinx, at a time when the social, legal, and political position of women was at a low ebb, is more than ironic.[62]

While I am not wholly convinced by Marcus's arguments regarding Wilde's characterization of Salome, as he depicts her as a cruel and murderous woman (who ultimately dies), it is worth noting her observation that "the decadent artist who depicted women as either 'the flower beneath the foot' or the destroying vampire (and these figures are the extreme embodiment of virgin and whore) were responding to the rumbles of discontent from European women."[63] Whereas Marcus is concerned here with how male decadent artists were using images of threatening women to assuage (their) anxiety about women who threatened to overturn gendered relations and norms, Jasmine Rault and Bridget Elliott have considered decadence as an aesthetic employed by nonheterosexual women artists and designers in the early twentieth century as a visual language that signified for them not only modernity, but also nonnormative sexualities.

If Salome was an icon of decadence, Beardsley was certainly perceived as one of the most "decadent" of British artists at the end of the nineteenth century. In a discussion of early-twentieth-century designers, Rault shows how Eileen Gray's interior designs were perceived as "decadent" by critics, at least in part because they saw a link between her work and Beardsley's illustrations. More importantly, the critics' use of the term "decadence" indicates anxieties not only about ornament and decoration in interior design by women, but also about the designers' (possible) sexual identities. As Rault notes, critics were "confused and disturbed" by Gray's "use of sensual decadence in otherwise distinctly modern designs." To "account for why her contemporaries may have been so troubled by this decadence, or why her incorporation of nineteenth-century aesthetic elements would have been so disturbing and suggestive of sexual perversions," Rault examines "the history in France of the relationship between decadence and interior design to show that it was structured by nineteenth-century theories of degeneration."[64]

In her book *Eileen Gray and the Design of Sapphic Modernity* (2011), Rault points out that in 1972, one writer compared Gray's early work to Beardsley's illustrations.[65] She also alludes to Elaine Showalter's assertion that in the late nineteenth century "decadence" was a "euphemism for [male] homosexuality,"[66] and Rault argues that by the 1920s decadence stood "for the aesthetic, moral, physical and sexual degeneration that modern architecture was explicitly designed to cure."[67] Jane Beckett has noted the relationships between ideas of excess, decoration, and decorum for women in the early twentieth century. She remarks that "excessiveness or decorativeness would have resulted from failure to achieve a necessary decorum in either elements or meaning. Decorum settles around concepts of seemliness and propriety, entailing ideas proper to the occasion, person or event, and thus becoming the opposite of excess."[68] Beckett highlights the fact that for women artists and designers, excess could signify as failure in terms of *both* gender and aesthetics.

Rault goes on to argue that in the early twentieth century, "women artists and writers were strategically appropriating elements of by then archaic nineteenth-century aesthetics as means for imagining female same-sex desire."[69] The difference between Rault's argument and my own arguments in *Radical Decadence* is that while early-twentieth-century female designers may have been self-reflexively adopting the visual language of *fin-de-siècle* decadence, including visuals that recall Beardsley's illustrations for *Salomé*, the artists whom I discuss in the following chapters are not explicitly referencing late-nineteenth-century decadence, nor would they necessarily conceive of their work as "decadent," although, as Rault argues for Gray's use of decadent aesthetics, I propose that the artists discussed in this study are deliberately *exceeding* norms related to gender and sexuality, whether they identify as heterosexual or lesbian. In other words, radical decadence is the theoretical apparatus that I employ to read these works, rather than a deliberate aesthetic choice on the part of the artists.

Rault draws on Bridget Elliott's earlier scholarship, noting that Elliott published the first article to consider the role that sexuality played in Gray's creative production.[70] Elliott has also discussed artists Romaine Brooks and Gluck in relation to decadent aesthetics. In one article, Elliott considers why Gluck and Brooks "chose to rework a highly self-conscious cult of artifice which was first celebrated in the aesthetic and decadent movements of the 1880s and 1890s rather than engaging with a more contemporary avant-garde rhetoric."[71] In order to answer this question, Elliott cites David Weir, who argues that "decadence should be understood not as a period of transition (during the 1890s from late-Victorian to modern), but as a dynamics of interference involving a reformation of aesthetic codes that can take place in any period."[72] If we take seriously Weir's vision of decadence as not restricted to the late nineteenth century, and not so much an aesthetic as a sexed and gendered (and raced) *act* of interference, then the works considered in this book fit that framework. They are not decadent "merely" because of their materials or content. They are decadent because they interfere with a range of understandings, beliefs, and ideologies related to both women and art.

Conclusion

Radical Decadence is the first book to treat the term, concept, aesthetic, and lived experience (or act) of decadence as an analytical framework for contemporary feminist art generally and for contemporary feminist art that employs materials historically associated with "craft" specifically. It is not, however, the first text to consider craft in relation to decadence. In 1999, the Craft Council Gallery in London organized the exhibition *Decadence? Views from the Edge of the Century*, which was reviewed negatively by at least one critic at the time.[73] In a review of the exhibition, Lesley Jackson remarked:

> As I was walking round the show, I kept thinking of alternative titles: *Self Indulgence*, *Strange Bedfellows* and *English Eccentrics* were three I came up with. I also kept thinking of ways in which the subject of decadence, which is potentially fascinating, could have been tackled in a [sic] such a way as to give the exhibition more meaning: by exploring the nature of obsession in greater depth, for example; or by contrasting the opposing forces of what Ettore Sottsass has described as "Minimalism" and "Maximalism."[74]

The fact that the exhibition's curators included a question mark in their title indicates that they too may have felt ambivalence, even hesitation, regarding the use of the term "decadence" as an organizing principle for the exhibition. I would speculate that this is because of lingering doubts about the acceptability of "decadence" as either an aesthetic or a behavior. "Self-indulgence," after all, has deeply moralizing significations, and "obsession" has its own set of negative connotations. Furthermore, neither term, I would argue, is synonymous with "decadence." It is worth noting here that in Orly Cogan's depiction of young women eating cupcakes and snorting cocaine, *Bittersweet Obsession* (Plate 2), she uses the word "obsession" in her title, rather than "addiction." This is important on the one hand because drug use is not necessarily indicative of addiction, and Cogan is disrupting some of the expectations revolving around (women's) illicit drug use, but it is also clearly a deliberate choice to play with the fact that this kind of language is often employed when describing behaviors that are perceived as "excessive."[75] Jackson's review underscores this fact.

Moving away from moralizing visions of decadence and excess, I propose that decadence, or more accurately, radical decadence, is a productive framework for the study of feminist textiles and craft that address issues related to consumption, drug use, female sexuality, self-fashioning, and "excessive" living more generally. By "excessive" I mean behaviors, identities, and quantities (or qualities) that are deemed "in excess" of that which is considered acceptable for women in any given city, culture, country, or context. In other words, "excess" is contingent. As Mary Russo argues in *The Female Grotesque*, "excess" is relative, and it needs something (the "norm") to exceed.[76] I have written elsewhere that excess is not, and has never been, a neutral concept.[77] The artists discussed in this book are aware of that fact. More to the point, excess and decadence are not synonymous, but they do overlap as concepts.

These overarching themes—decadence, excess—which are evident in recent feminist textile art, are reconsidered as *radically* decadent, not in a pejorative sense, but rather in terms of self-reflexivity, refusal, and agency. Decadence in the late nineteenth century was associated with rich textiles, drug and alcohol consumption, and nonnormative sexualities. In this book, I define "decadence" as both an aesthetic and lived experience of excess, that is to say, the exceeding of gendered, sexed, and raced norms related to both women and art. Drawing on late-nineteenth-century definitions of "decadence," as well as on the works discussed in this book, I would add that decadence is an aesthetic concerned with, among other things, artifice, luxury, clothing, morbidity, pleasure, and for some decadents (both past and present), the consumption of drugs and alcohol. According to Talia Schaffer and Kathy Alexis Psomiades, "Decadence, with its fascination with the unnatural, death, decay, the body, and the exotic other, continued aestheticism's interest in artifice, intense experience, the mixing of beauty and strangeness, and the desire to experience life itself as art."[78] Linda Dowling notes in her study of literary decadence and language that what is most useful in previous texts on decadence is the "idea of Decadence as counterpoetics and critique," which "possesses wherever it occurs a genuine power of illumination."[79] In what follows, decadence, or more precisely, *radical decadence*, is considered as a critical feminist approach to both creative production and lived experience that necessarily entails risks and failures, deliberate or otherwise.[80]

Notes

1 Janis Jefferies, "Contemporary Textiles: The Art Fabric," in Nadine Monem (ed.), *Contemporary Textiles: The Fabric of Fine Art* (London: Black Dog Publishing, 2008), 46.

2 Svetlana Alpers, "Art History and Its Exclusions: The Example of Dutch Art," in Norma Broude and Mary D. Garrard (eds), *Feminism and Art History: Questioning the Litany* (New York: Harper & Row, 1982), 188.

3 Rozsika Parker, *The Subversive Stitch: Embroidery and the Making of the Feminine* (1984; London and New York: I. B. Tauris, 2010), 5.

4 Rozsika Parker and Griselda Pollock, *Old Mistresses: Women, Art and Ideology* (London: Routledge and Kegan Paul, 1981), 58.

5 See, for instance, Rosemary Betterton, *An Intimate Distance: Women, Artists and the Body* (New York and London: Routledge, 1996); Carol Duncan, *The Aesthetics of Power: Essays in Critical Art History* (Cambridge: Cambridge University Press, 1993); Janice Helland, *The Studios of Frances and Margaret MacDonald* (New York: St Martin's Press, 1996); Kristina Huneault, *Difficult Subjects: Working Women and Visual Culture, Britain 1880-1914* (Aldershot, UK, and Burlington, VT: Ashgate, 2002); Janis Jefferies, "Loving Attention: An Outburst of Craft in Contemporary Art," in Maria Elena Buszek (ed.), *Extra/Ordinary: Craft and Contemporary Art* (Durham, NC, and London: Duke University Press, 2011), 222–40; Lynda Nead, *Myths of Sexuality: Representations of Women in Victorian Britain* (Oxford: Basil Blackwell, 1990); Linda Nochlin, *Women, Art, and Power and Other Essays* (New York: Harper and Row, 1988); Griselda Pollock, *Vision and Difference: Femininity, Feminism and Histories of Art* (New York and London: Routledge, 1988).

6 Allyson Mitchell (ed.), "A Call to Arms," in *When Women Rule the World: Judy Chicago in Thread* (Toronto: Textile Museum of Canada, 2009), 18. For more on the history of *The Dinner Party* and its reception, see Rachel Dickson (ed.), "Introduction," in *Judy Chicago and Louise Bourgeois, Helen Chadwick, Tracey Emin* (London: Lund Humphries, 2012), 8–13.

7 Janis Jefferies, "Textiles," in Fiona Carson and Claire Pajaczkowska (eds), *Feminist Visual Culture* (New York and London: Routledge, 2001), 191.

8 Alexandra Kokoli, "'Not a Straight Line but a Spiral': Charting Continuity and Change in Textiles Informed by Feminism," *Image & Text* 23 (2014), 115.

9 For a discussion of materiality and how certain materials have been employed as sites of resistance and (feminine) "excess," see Giuliana Bruno, *Surface: Matters of Aesthetics, Materiality, and Media* (Chicago: University of Chicago Press, 2014); Janis Jefferies, Diana Wood Conroy, and Hazel Clark (eds), *The Handbook of Textile Culture* (London: Bloomsbury, 2016); and T'ai Smith, *Bauhaus Weaving Theory: From Feminine Craft to Mode of Design* (Minneapolis and London: University of Minnesota Press, 2014), xv, xx.

10 On the importance of stories for feminist theory, see Clare Hemmings, *Why Stories Matter: The Political Grammar of Feminist Theory* (Durham, NC, and London: Duke University Press, 2011).

11 On Ringgold's story quilts, see Thalia Gouma-Peterson, "Faith Ringgold's Journey: From Greek Busts to African Dilemma Tales," in Dan Cameron (ed.), *Faith Ringgold's French Collection and Other Story Quilts* (New York: New Museum of Contemporary Art, 1998), 39–48; bell hooks, "Aesthetic Inheritances: History Worked by Hand," in Joan Livingstone and John Ploof (eds), *The Object of Labour: Art, Cloth, and Cultural Production* (Chicago: School of the Art Institute of Chicago Press, 2007), 326–32; Freida High W. Tesfagiorgis, "Afrofemcentrism and its Fruition in the Art of Elizabeth Catlett and Faith Ringgold," in Norma Broude and Mary D. Garrard (eds), *The Expanding Discourse: Feminism and Art History* (New York: HarperCollins, 1992), 475–85; and Michele Wallace (ed.), *Faith Ringgold: Twenty Years of Painting, Sculpture and Performance (1963-1983)* (New York: Studio Museum in Harlem, 1984). On quilting, see Patricia Mainardi, "Quilts: The Great American Art," in Broude and Garrard (eds), *Feminism and Art History: Questioning the Litany*, 330–46.

12 Jefferies, "Contemporary Textiles," 38.

13 Norma Broude, "Miriam Schapiro and 'Femmage': Reflections on the Conflict Between Decoration and Abstraction in Twentieth-Century Art," in Broude and Garrard (eds), *Feminism and Art History: Questioning the Litany*, 315–29.

14 Mitchell, "A Call to Arms," 15.

15 Ibid., 18.

16 Mary Russo, *The Female Grotesque: Risk, Excess and Modernity* (New York and London: Routledge, 1994), 10.

17 Edward Lucie-Smith, *Symbolist Art* (London: Thames and Hudson, 1993), 54.

18 Sociolinguists Adam Jaworski and Nikolas Coupland define "discourse" as "language use relative to social, political and cultural formations . . . language reflecting social order but also language shaping social order, and shaping individuals' interaction with society." Quoted in Christine Ross, *The Aesthetics of Disengagement: Contemporary Art and Depression* (Minneapolis and London: University of Minnesota Press, 2006), xxv.

19 Alice Echols, *Daring to Be Bad: Radical Feminism in America 1967-1975* (Minneapolis: University of Minnesota Press, 1989).

20 Alexandra Kokoli, "Introduction: Looking On, Bouncing Back," in Alexandra M. Kokoli (ed.), *Feminism Reframed* (Newcastle, UK: Cambridge Scholars Publishing, 2008), 3.

21 Jayne Wark, *Radical Gestures: Feminism and Performance Art in North America* (Montreal and Kingston: McGill-Queen's University Press, 2006), 5.

22 Ibid., 3–4.

23 Kokoli, "Introduction," 7.

24 Griselda Pollock, "What is it that Feminist Interventions Do? Feminism and Difference in Retrospect and Prospect," in Kokoli (ed.), *Feminism Reframed*, 255.

25 Linda Dowling, "The Decadent and the New Woman in the 1890's," *Nineteenth-Century Fiction* 33, no. 4 (March 1979): 436.

26 Ibid., 447.

27	On the *femme fatale* in late-nineteenth-century France, see Elizabeth K. Menon, "Decadent Addictions: Tobacco, Alcohol, Popular Imagery, and Café Culture in France," in Laurinda S. Dixon (ed.), with the assistance of Gabriel P. Weisberg, *In Sickness and in Health: Disease as Metaphor in Art and Popular Wisdom* (Newark: University of Delaware Press, 2004), 101–24. On the New Woman in late-nineteenth-century France, see Mary Louise Roberts, *Disruptive Acts: The New Woman in Fin-de-Siècle France* (Chicago: University of Chicago Press, 2002). The relationship between France and England in the context of decadence is articulated by Richard Gilman when he states: "The 'Yellow Nineties,' which make up the English counterpart of the *fin de siècle* in France, were given the provocative name through a chance circumstance: the exotic French novels that had begun to have a vogue in London during the previous decade happened to have been bound mostly in that color." He goes on to discuss the decadent journal *The Yellow Book* (1894–97), to which Aubrey Beardsley contributed illustrations. Richard Gilman, *Decadence: The Strange Life of an Epithet* (New York: Farrar, Straus and Giroux, 1975), 114–15.

28	See, for example, Lucie-Smith, *Symbolist Art*; Bram Dijkstra, *Idols of Perversity: Fantasies of Feminine Evil in Fin-de-Siècle Culture* (Oxford: Oxford University Press, 1986); and Philippe Jullian, *Dreamers of Decadence: Symbolist Painters of the 1890s* (New York: Praeger Publishers, 1971).

29	See Michael Hatt, "Space, Surface, Self: Homosexuality and the Aesthetic Interior," *Visual Culture in Britain* 8, no. 1 (Summer 2007): 105–28. See also Ruth Temple, "Truth in Labelling: Pre-Raphaelitism, Aestheticism, Decadence, Fin de Siècle," *ELT* 17 (1974): 201–22.

30	Kimberly Wahl, *Dressed as in a Painting: Women and British Aestheticism in an Age of Reform* (Durham and New Hampshire: University of New Hampshire Press, 2013), xxix.

31	Sandra Siegel, "Literature and Degeneration: The Representation of 'Decadence,'" in Edward Chamberlin and Sander L. Gilman (eds), *Degeneration: The Dark Side of Progress* (New York: Columbia University Press, 1985), 208.

32	George L. Mosse, "Masculinity and the Decadence," in Roy Porter and Mikuláš Teich (eds), *Sexual Knowledge, Sexual Science: The History of Attitudes to Sexuality* (Cambridge: Cambridge University Press, 1994), 254.

33	Lynda Nead, *Victorian Babylon: People, Streets, and Images in Nineteenth-Century London* (New Haven and London: Yale University Press, 2000).

34	On the representation of female morphine users in literature, see Susan Zieger, "'How Far am I Responsible?': Women and Morphinomania in Late-Nineteenth-Century Britain", *Victorian Studies* 48, no. 1 (Autumn 2005): 59–81.

35	Gilman, *Decadence*, 5.

36	Ibid.

37	Elaine Showalter, *Sexual Anarchy: Gender and Culture at the Fin de Siècle* (London: Bloomsbury, 1991), 169.

38	Martin Green, *Children of the Sun: A Narrative of "Decadence" in England After 1918* (New York: Basic Books, 1976).

39	Linda Dowling, *Language and Decadence in the Victorian Fin de Siècle* (Princeton, NJ: Princeton University Press, 1986), ix.

40	According to the editors of a book on the aesthetics and politics of decadence: "Although critics may distance themselves from the 'improper' but strangely overproductive nonreproduction to which they attribute the origin and dissemination of decadence, an interesting reversal takes place when these critics treat the relationship of *so-called decadent women writers* to the predominantly male literary phenomenon. For here the familial metaphors that, as we have seen, generally brand the male decadents as figurative deviations from the norms of 'healthy' heterosexual procreation, seem instead to present decadent women as products of the very family structure their male counterparts ostensibly threaten." Liz Constable, Matthew Potolsky, and Dennis Denisoff, "Introduction," in Liz Constable, Dennis Denisoff, and Matthew Potolsky (eds), *Perennial Decay: On the Aesthetics and Politics of Decadence* (Philadelphia: University of Pennsylvania Press, 1999), 6–7. Emphasis added. Elaine Showalter has edited a collection of New Women writers who she discusses in relation to decadence, but as she notes in the Introduction, "The decadent artist was invariably male, and decadence, as a hyper-aesthetic movement, defined itself against the feminine and biological creativity of women." Elaine Showalter, "Introduction," in Elaine Showalter (ed.), *Daughters of Decadence: Women Writers of the Fin-de-Siècle* (London: Virago, 1993), x.

41　Rita Felski, *The Gender of Modernity* (Cambridge, MA, and London: Harvard University Press, 1995), 20.

42　Ibid., 62.

43　Russo, *The Female Grotesque*, 24.

44　See, among many others, Parker, *The Subversive Stitch*.

45　Cheryl Buckley, "Ceramics," in Carson and Pajaczkowska (eds), *Feminist Visual Culture*, 171.

46　Ibid., 183.

47　Quoted in Claudette Lauzon, "What the Body Remembers: Rebecca Belmore's Memorial to Missing Women," in Olivier Asselin, Johanne Lamoureux, and Christine Ross (eds), *Precarious Visualities: New Perspectives on Identification in Contemporary Art and Visual Culture* (Montreal and Kingston: McGill-Queen's University Press, 2008), 160. See Peggy Phelan, *Unmarked: The Politics of Performance* (New York and London: Routledge, 1993), 10.

48　Jefferies, "Textiles," 198.

49　Naomi Schor, *Reading in Detail: Aesthetics and the Feminine* (1987; New York and London: Routledge, 2007), 45–46.

50　Quoted in Ellen Rooney, "Foreword: An Aesthetic of Bad Objects," in Naomi Schor (ed.), *Reading in Detail: Aesthetics and the Feminine* (1987; New York and London: Routledge, 2007), xv.

51　Ibid., xvi.

52　Quoted in ibid., xvii.

53　For further discussion, see Anne Anlin Cheng, *Second Skin: Josephine Baker and the Modern Surface* (Oxford and New York: Oxford University Press, 2011), 24.

54　Bridget Elliott and Janice Helland, "Introduction," in Bridget Elliott and Janice Helland (eds), *Women Artists and the Decorative Arts, 1880-1935: The Gender of Ornament* (Aldershot, UK, and Burlington, VT: Ashgate, 2002), 3.

55　Quoted in Rooney, "Foreword," xviii.

56　Ibid., xix. Schor writes in *Reading in Detail*: "For the archeology of the detail, the sexism of rhetoric is of crucial significance. Neo-classical aesthetics is imbued with the residues of the rhetorical imaginary, a sexist imaginary where the ornamental is inevitably bound up with the feminine, when it is not the pathological—two notions Western culture has throughout its history had a great deal of trouble distinguishing. This imaginary femininity weighs heavily on the fate of the detail as well as of the ornament in aesthetics, burdening them with the negative connotations of the feminine: the decorative, the natural, the impure, and the monstrous" (49).

57　See also Jonah Siegel, *Desire and Excess: The Nineteenth-Century Culture of Art* (Princeton: Princeton University Press, 2000).

58 Jane Marcus, *Art and Anger: Reading Like a Woman* (Columbus: Ohio State University Press, 1988), xix.

59 Quoted in ibid., 13. Serendipitously, while I was writing this Introduction, I was given a book entitled *Masterworks of Ukiyo-E: "The Decadents"* by Jūzō Suzuki and Isaburō Oka, trans. John Bester (Tokyo, Japan, and Palo Alto, CA: Kodansha International Ltd., 1969), which supports Wilde's view of Beardsley's illustration. The relationship between Beardsley and Japanese art has been investigated in Linda Gertner Zatlin, *Beardsley, Japonisme, and the Perversion of the Victorian Ideal* (Cambridge: Cambridge University Press, 1997).

60 Marcus, *Art and Anger*, 3.

61 See Rosemary Betterton, "'A Perfect Woman': The Political Body of Suffrage," in *An Intimate Distance: Women, Artists and the Body*, 46–78.

62 Marcus, *Art and Anger*, 4.

63 Ibid., 8.

64 Jasmine Rault, *Eileen Gray and the Design of Sapphic Modernity: Staying In* (Farnham, UK, and Burlington, VT: Ashgate, 2011), 29.

65 Ibid., 17. Rault also refers to "the richly textured sensuality of materials (lacquer, inlaid silver with silver and mother-of-pearl arabesques at the rue de Lota apartment, thick, hand-dyed, hand-woven wool carpets, throw rugs and blankets made of fur and silk)" that speak to the decadence of Gray's interior designs (17).

66 Ibid., 17. See Showalter, *Sexual Anarchy*, 171.

67 Rault, *Eileen Gray*, 17.

68 Jane Beckett, "Engendering the Spaces of Modernity: The Women's Exhibition, Amsterdam 1913," in Elliott and Helland (eds), *Women Artists and the Decorative Arts, 1880-1935: The Gender of Ornament*, 161.

69 Rault, *Eileen Gray*, 17.

70 Ibid., 9. See Bridget Elliott, "Housing the Work: Women Artists, Modernism and the *maison d'artiste*: Eileen Gray, Romaine Brooks and Gluck," in Bridget Elliott and Janice Helland (eds), *Women Artists and the Decorative Arts 1880-1935: The Gender of Ornament* (Aldershot, UK, and Burlington, VT: Ashgate, 2002), 176–91.

71 Bridget Elliott, "Performing the Picture or Painting the Other: Romaine Brooks, Gluck and the Question of Decadence in 1923," in Katy Deepwell (ed.), *Women Artists and Modernism* (Manchester and New York: Manchester University Press, 1998), 76.

72 Ibid. Weir notes that "most of the writers discussed in this book are male, and most of them are misogynistic in the extreme." David Weir, *Decadence and the Making of Modernism* (Amherst: University of Massachusetts Press, 1995), xiv.

73 There was no exhibition catalogue in the traditional sense. A limited edition pack of cards with quotations related to decadence on each card was sold as an unorthodox catalogue. *Decadence? Views from the Edge of the Century*, Crafts Council Gallery, London N1, January 21 to March 14, 1999. The exhibition's three curators were textile historian Mary Schoeser, Philip Hughes, Director of the Ruthin Gallery, and Louise Taylore from the Crafts Council. Louise Pratt and Beatrice Hosegood wrote in their "Introduction" (on the Joker card): "*Decadence?* takes place at the start of 1999 and eavesdrops on the debate about our likes, loves and desires, our hopes and fears in the late twentieth century. Twenty outstanding makers have been asked to show their work about decadence in the 1990s. They have made objects with which to indulge ourselves. It is an occasion for luxury and subtle excess. But behind the fun and flamboyance lie some timely observations on our ways of life." Stephen Calloway (Curator Prints and Drawings V&A) is quoted on one of the playing cards: "The Decadent, one might imagine, would have little time for Crafts or Councils. And yet, the Decadent in our time is a Dandy and a Connoisseur of the Beautiful, the Perverse, the Sensual and the Obscure. The true Decadent delights in the Rare, in those things which have Style, and above all in the Artificial; who then but the Decadent will truly value the work of the cunning Artificer?" Jeweler Ingeborg Bratman, whose contribution to the exhibition was a 12-foot string of pearls produced in 1998, is also quoted. On the Ace card, Bratman defines decadence as "deliberately shocking and a precursor to puritanism or severe restraint; risqué, louche, sensuous, voluptuous, tactile, blousy, over-confident, satin and velvet, opium and absinthe; gold *isn't*, but being painted with gold *is*."

74 Unidentified clipping, National Art Library, Special Collections.

75 For more on this, see Julia Skelly, *Wasted Looks: Addiction and British Visual Culture, 1751-1919* (Farnham, UK, and Burlington, VT: Ashgate, 2014), 6–7.

76 Russo, *The Female Grotesque*.

77 Julia Skelly, "Introduction: The Uses of Excess," in Julia Skelly (ed.), *The Uses of Excess in Visual and Material Culture, 1600-2010* (Farnham, UK, and Burlington, VT: Ashgate, 2014), 1.

78 Talia Schaffer and Kathy Alexis Psomiades, "Introduction," in Talia Schaffer and Kathy Alexis Psomiades (eds), *Women and British Aestheticism* (Charlottesville and London: University of Virginia Press, 1999), 3.

79 Dowling, *Language and Decadence in the Victorian Fin de Siècle*, x.

80 Jack Halberstam asks: "What kinds of reward can failure offer us? Perhaps most obviously, failure allows us to escape the punishing norms that discipline behavior and manage human development with the goal of delivering us from unruly childhoods to orderly and predictable adulthoods. Failure preserves some of the wondrous anarchy of childhood and disturbs the supposedly clean boundaries between adults and children, winners and losers. And while failure certainly comes accompanied by a host of negative affects, such as disappointment, disillusionment, and despair, it also provides the opportunity to use these negative affects to poke holes in the toxic positivity of contemporary life." Judith (Jack) Halberstam, *The Queer Art of Failure* (Durham, NC, and London: Duke University Press, 2011), 3.

1

CONSUMING CRAFT, CUPCAKES, AND COCAINE: ORLY COGAN, SHANE WALTENER, AND SHELLEY MILLER

Drugs and decadence

A range of commentators associated drug use with decadence in the late nineteenth century.[1] According to Fraser Harrison in his study of decadent male artists associated with the *Yellow Book* in the 1890s, "The threats and demands represented by the ever accelerating movement towards female emancipation on all fronts, seem to have unnerved and unbalanced this group of men and driven them to seek comfort and oblivion in homosexuality, prostitution, addiction to alcohol and opiates, sterile relationships with children, and, in some cases, forlorn celibacy."[2] Max Nordau famously linked drug use with degeneration, and degeneration with decadence, pointing to Oscar Wilde as evidence that decadence led to racial degeneration.[3] Both Harrison and Nordau focused exclusively, as was typical in the late nineteenth century, on the relationship between decadence and nonnormative masculinity generally, or in relation to specific male individuals, and Harrison's statement in particular demonstrates that at least some male decadents felt threatened by the suffrage movement. Harrison therefore positions decadence as a male style or approach to life that was inextricably tied to the perception of certain women as threatening to gendered norms. I open with a discussion of decadence and drugs, because one of the artists discussed in this chapter, Orly Cogan, has produced textile artworks depicting women consuming cocaine. I also want to underscore the fact that decadence was historically associated with male artists who represented (and felt threatened by) women. *Radical Decadence* departs from this vision of decadence in focusing primarily on women artists who are themselves transgressing various gendered, sexed, and raced norms.[4]

This chapter explores intersections between current fiber art practices and social practices, as well as the concomitant desire for community. Through the case studies of Israel-born, New York-based artist Orly Cogan's work, and Belgian artist Shane Waltener's participatory workshops involving both knitting and cake decorating, I want to suggest that there are hitherto untheorized intersections between the production and consumption of crafts, baked goods, and drugs that revolve around a desire for community and human connection. Further to this, all of these social practices—crafting and the consumption of drugs and baked goods—are often characterized by repetition, pleasure, obsession, and shame. Although it may not be immediately apparent how crafting can be "shameful"—and I would be quick to clarify that none of these activities are *innately* shameful, but are related to shame through complex sociocultural discourses—I want to refer to the text that concludes *The Craft Reader* (2010), entitled "The Politics of Craft: A Roundtable." Art historian Julia Bryan-Wilson, who chaired the roundtable (it took place in fall 2007), notes that she had recently attended the "Craft at the Limits" conference at the Getty, where some scholars— as opposed to craft practitioners—had talked about craft as "embarrassing." Liz Collins, an artist who works with textiles, responded to this comment with the succinct phrase, "Craft Shame."[5] The notion of "craft shame," of course, exists because of the art/craft hierarchy. It is because of the insidiousness of that ostensible hierarchy, which has been deconstructed by scholars such as Rozsika Parker, Griselda Pollock, and Janis Jefferies,[6] among others, that there could still be so-called "craft shame" in the twenty-first century. My point is that all three activities that I am concerned with in this chapter have more in common than might appear at first glance. On a very basic level, the making of textiles and baked goods, and the consumption of narcotics, are related through their repetitive acts: one stitch at a time; reading and rereading a recipe; taking a drug again and again. I suggest that there is sometimes a thin line between "acceptable" social practices such as cake making and quilting bees, and illicit social practices such as drug consumption. Ultimately, this chapter sets out to query the many registers of meaning that are illuminated when we consider Waltener's participatory art against Cogan's textile works that represent women consuming cupcakes and cocaine. The latter half of the chapter examines Cogan's work in relation to Mary Russo's "female grotesque" and Barbara Creed's "monstrous feminine," both excessive female figures that threaten the social order through abject consumption and embrace failure in their rejection of perfection.

The promise of community: Craft, cake, and cocaine

One of the threads that link the consumption of craft, cakes, and cocaine is the desire for community. As Maria Elena Buszek has observed: "The sensuous, tactile 'information' of craft media speaks . . . of a direct connection to humanity that is perhaps endangered, or at the very least being rapidly reconfigured in our technologically saturated, twenty-first-century lives."[7] This perception of craft and crafting has led some textile artists to engage with "participatory" or relational art practices. In *Artificial Hells: Participatory Art and the Politics of Spectatorship* (2012), Claire Bishop investigates the "surge of artistic interest in participation and collaboration that has taken place since the early 1990s, and in a multitude of global locations,"[8] but she also demonstrates that participation has long been a trait of avant-garde art, albeit on the margins of "mainstream" art-making. Participatory art is often discussed in terms of social activism, and this continues to be the case for participatory craft-making practices. Current "craftivist" practices are part of a lineage that includes the production of suffrage banners by female producers in the late nineteenth and early twentieth centuries, and the Arts and Crafts movement in Britain.[9] In what follows, I discuss one example of participatory art, Shane Waltener's cake decorating workshop *Sweet Nothings*, in relation to Orly Cogan's textile works that represent women consuming both cupcakes and cocaine (see Plate 2 and Figure 1.1). I want to illuminate some of the intersections between crafting, baking, and drug-taking as practices that can be isolating as well as community-building, shameful as well as pleasurable, thus destabilizing not only the notion that participatory crafting practices are straightforward processes that necessarily result in human connection, but also the belief that the consumption of illicit drugs—such as cocaine—is necessarily a shameful behavior engaged in privately for fear of legal, social, and physiological repercussions.[10]

London-based, Belgian textile artist Shane Waltener has created participatory and collaborative contexts for both knitting and cake decorating. For instance, he has organized several knitting circles in galleries.[11] According to Waltener,

> My work is about celebrating and rediscovering craft and addressing the balance between art and craft. Knitting with elastic thread allows me to create monumental pieces that challenge the architecture and authority of a given space. The knitting performances I create are about the social aspect of the craft. They are less about the piece being produced than about the exchange between participants. Each stitch contains a thought and these are entered onto a network (the knitted loop) and passed around by all the knitters in the circle. The loop is then exhibited as a document tracing the history of the event.[12]

Figure 1.1 Orly Cogan, *Cupcake Girl*, 2005. Courtesy of the artist.

Waltener's performance/workshop *Sweet Nothings: An Intimate History of Cake Making* (2005) created an "activated space"[13] in which the ritual of cake making was illuminated as a creative process and social practice comparable to knitting circles, quilting bees, and the production of textile objects, such as banners, by nineteenth-century suffragettes and temperance advocates.[14] Janis Jefferies has previously examined Waltener's performative work in terms of relational aesthetics, according to which the artist is positioned as facilitator rather than as "maker."[15]

Contrary to the arguments that position crafting as a potentially social and community-building activity, Bradley Quinn suggests that "embroidery, as a solitary craft . . . evokes a sense of emotional isolation. Rather than building bridges between textile practice and art, it can also present an eerie sense of dislocation and unease."[16] Yet artists such as Waltener have demonstrated that contemporary textile practices also provide opportunities for community-building and human connection. Waltener's *Sweet Nothings* dealt in cakes rather than textiles, but the objective was still the facilitation of social relationships. The cake-decorating performative workshop was part of the show *Ceremony*, which was cocurated by Sandra Ross and the radical knitter Freddie Robbins. According to Jefferies, *Ceremony* brought together "an eclectic range of works, performances, and projects that explored the performative relationship between object and ritual."[17] Jefferies notes that participants experimented with icing and cake-decorating techniques, creating "brightly colored, lush cakes" that the participants of the workshop also ate.[18] Within this context, baked goods signified as part of happy domestic rituals and "rites of passage."[19] A photograph of participants (notably all males, thereby destabilizing the gendered stereotype of the domestic goddess who bakes) shows them sitting around a table, heads bowed, focused, intent on their respective icing projects. Although Jefferies notes that *Sweet Nothings* "opened up a space of conversation as the cakes were made and decorated,"[20] the intensity with which the five men ice their cakes creates an image of self-contained, solitary acts occurring side by side.[21]

The failure of this photograph to adequately capture the intersubjective nature of *Sweet Nothings* speaks to the problematics of still images and participatory art. As Claire Bishop has stated: "To grasp participatory art from images alone is almost impossible: casual photographs of people talking, eating, attending a workshop or screening or seminar tell us very little, almost nothing, about the concept and context of a given project. They rarely provide more than fragmentary evidence, and convey nothing of the affective dynamic that propels artists to make these projects and people to participate in them."[22] Another photograph documenting the products of *Sweet Nothings* shows a plethora of colorful cakes on paper plates, eclectically iced. In the center of the photograph is a plate piled high with cakes of various shapes and a mishmash of decorative icing styles. The cakes cannot be said to be particularly appetizing, aesthetically speaking, but that was surely not the point of the exercise. In Waltener's view, his participatory projects allow for visitors to "get a chance, for a sustained period of time, to reflect on what they are doing while engaging with a creative process, be it knitting, cake decorating, or some other craft technique. This creates an opportunity to ponder on what they have seen, what their connection is with any given craft technique, share it with others, and make it relevant to their own understanding of art and craft."[23]

One of the objectives of *Sweet Nothings*, namely to produce a space in which human relationships could form and evolve, is completely erased by the photograph of the cakes; there are no human agents present, only the fruits of their labors. Furthermore, the often complex relationship between eater and baked good is also erased in the photographs taken of Waltener's workshop. The images cannot capture ambivalence or shame or regret about consuming a piece or pieces of cake. Feminist scholars from a range of disciplines have discussed baked goods in relation to bulimia, shame, ambivalence, and fetishization, particularly in terms of women's consumption. As Lorraine Gamman and Merja Makinen have commented, "A woman having an excessive relationship with a cream cake is seen as deficient in her femininity."[24] However, Waltener is a male artist, and in the photograph documenting the cake-making workshop, all of the participants are male. It is unlikely that women did not participate, but this particular photograph captures men hunched over their cakes, decorating away. The work then, and the photographs that are the performance's afterlife, undermine the traditional gendering of cakes as a "feminine" food and, at the same time, a source of a particularly "feminine" kind of shame.

Like some of the photographs that documented *Sweet Nothings*, Orly Cogan's installation *Confections* of 2006 comprises baked goods set out on a table (Plate 4).[25] Allison James has observed that "confectionary is conceptually *both* food and non-food, an ambiguous substance and, as such, is replete with ritual significance."[26] The photograph of *Confections* shows a rectangular table covered in a red-and-white checkered tablecloth upon which sit a plethora of baked goods. Whereas the cakes produced as part of the *Sweet Nothings* performance were characterized by their imperfections and amateurish application of icing, the foodstuffs in *Confections* are notable for their perfection. These baked goods look too good to eat, and indeed they are. Each pastry in *Confections* is a life-size hand-crafted object made out of fiber-based materials, paper, and paint.[27] There are no human subjects present, no social relationships being facilitated. The cakes, cupcakes, and pies are displayed as though waiting for a social gathering to unfold around them, but there will be no consumption here, except of the optical kind. The installation, then, evokes a party that no one attended, a failed social event with the uneaten cakes as evidence of their maker's isolation.

Cogan does, however, represent the consumption of baked goods in several of her textile works. In *Bittersweet Obsession* (Plate 2), two young women in the foreground eat cupcakes, though one appears to have just taken the last bite and holds only a cup and saucer. In the center of this work, a woman cuts into a strawberry-covered cake while looking directly back at the viewer. At the top of the textile—above the two denim-clad women snorting cocaine—small female figures wearing aprons carry two huge iced cakes. The tiny aproned figure on the left appears as though she has two heads, and indeed could be considered as an example of the monstrous female body that recalls the Hydra and Medusa, one of the threatening women evoked by male decadent poets in the late nineteenth century.[28]

Cogan was born in Israel in 1971, and she is currently based in New York. She received her BFA from the Maryland Institute College of Art in Baltimore and has exhibited at the Elizabeth A. Sackler Center for Feminist Art at the Brooklyn Museum, among other important venues. Her work was included, for instance, in the immensely popular show

Pricked: Extreme Embroidery, which was held at New York's Museum of Arts and Design in 2007. Cogan often employs vintage fabrics associated with domesticity, such as tablecloths and bedsheets. She has remarked that "my work is an irreverent yet gentle take on the conventions of femininity. I stitch figures on dainty vintage linens, already embroidered by an earlier and more circumscribed generation of women."[29]

In *Bittersweet Obsession*, the women wearing aprons would seem to signify a kind of ironic 1950s domesticity situated in such close proximity to two young women snorting cocaine through straws or dollar bills. Rather than portraying all of these women together in order to create an image of human connection, Cogan has positioned each figure so as to create a subversive pattern that brings new meaning to Jefferies's remarks about patterns in fiber art:

> Detail, the minute and intricate attention to pattern, is acknowledged as having the potential to destabilise an internal ordering of surface structure. Detail participates in a larger semantic field, bonded on the one hand by the ornamental by its connotation of effeminacy and decadence, and on the other by the everyday, whose prissiness is rooted in the domestic sphere presided over by women.[30]

In *Bittersweet Obsession*, the consumption of both baked goods and cocaine are represented as solitary activities. This is also the case in works such as *Mirror, Mirror* (Plate 3) and *Cupcake Girl* (Figure 1.1). And yet, like crafting and baking, the consumption of illicit drugs is not always solitary. Indeed, as scholars such as Tom Yardley and Kane Race have argued, drug-taking is often predicated on a desire not only for pleasure but also for community and human connection. In an essay on craft communities, Dennis Stevens observes that "communities of practice are formed when social units are united by common areas of concerns or interests, interact regularly, share a common vocabulary, and, even without acknowledging it, learn with and from another in the process."[31] His definition could suffice for knitting circles, baking groups, or drug communities.

In *Pleasure Consuming Medicine: The Queer Politics of Drugs* (2009), Kane Race examines the use of drugs within gay communities, employing pleasure as a framework for his analysis. He observes that "drugs have been a significant part of these gay practices of transformation and self-creation—though it has been unclear how to grasp their activity."[32] He discusses the way that drugs have served myriad purposes within queer communities, which destabilizes the image of illicit drug use as deviant, criminal, immoral, and isolating. Race observes, for instance, that the "queer dance party is often seen as a sort of mass escape from the realities of queer life or else a scene of excessive consumerism. But I want to suggest that it had a series of effects that were more materially productive."[33] He argues, for instance, that ecstasy "was an active component in the effective community response to AIDS."[34] Rather than being an isolating, solitary, shameful activity, the consumption of illicit drugs such as ecstasy, Race proposes, served to build social relationships founded in agency and mutual support within the context of the AIDS crisis. Tom Yardley has also discussed the consumption of illicit drugs in terms of a desire for community and human connection. In his book *Why We Take Drugs: Seeking Excess and Communion in the Modern World* (2012), Yardley states: "The British cultural anthropologist Victor Turner, for example, has suggested that entry into a shared state in which the activities of everyday life are temporarily suspended can induce an intense sense of belonging or 'communitas' with others. This 'liminal' social space is created when the sensual reality of the participants is synchronized through shared physical experiences."[35] In this vein, Yardley employs the notion of "communitas" as a theoretical framework for his investigation into why human beings desire intoxication.[36] He concludes that "although intoxication in contemporary society often lacks the pageantry and ceremony associated with the creation of liminal encounters in earlier periods or other cultures, the ad hoc rituals of intoxication can be viewed as leading into a similar experiential space. This space, which is at once real and ideal, symbolic and material, is realized in the intoxicated body as it opens to the world and to others."[37] Yardley's analysis would therefore serve as a useful framework for thinking about Waltener's *Sweet Nothings*, as well as for the consumption of both licit and illicit addictive substances.

While both Race's and Yardley's discussions are significant for a radical reenvisioning of illicit drug use (which is, of course, distinct from addiction, and I deliberately avoid the phrase "drug abuse" in this book), their analyses are not primarily concerned with women drug users. Sociologist Elizabeth Ettore and policy scholar Susan C. Boyd, on the other hand, are concerned with the ways that the female drug user has been discursively produced, and how addiction discourses have had material impacts on female drug users in everyday life.[38] Significantly, craft has often been discussed as being inextricably tied to everyday life, and, indeed, Cogan's textile works such as *Bittersweet Obsession* unveil the fact that some women consume both baked goods and illicit drugs in their day-to-day lives. She does not, however, portray these activities as community based, although that in no way obscures the fact that women consume both baked goods and illegal drugs in groups and as part of communities.[39] In what follows, I set out to demonstrate the ways in which Cogan's textile works that represent women consuming cocaine and cupcakes subvert a range of ideologies and stereotypes related to illicit drug use, women's relationship with food, and the image of the consuming woman as grotesque and excessive.

Women, craft, and consumption

In their book *By Hand: The Use of Craft in Contemporary Art* (2007), Shu Hung and Joseph Magliaro comment that "an awareness of environmental sustainability and a disavowal of mass consumption are themes in the larger context of handmade work."[40] Scholars such as Kirsty Robertson have discussed the many ways in which contemporary textile artists are concerned with resisting mass consumption and consumer culture in the Western world. As Robertson observes, "For activist knitters . . . knitting is seen as a radical alternative to the commodification of all aspects of life."[41] *Radical Decadence* departs from this framing of craft. This and other chapters in the book are very much concerned with how women consume and how women's consumption is represented, erased, or alluded to in contemporary feminist textiles and craft. Several feminist scholars have focused on consumption as a productive framework for considering women's agency. According to Rita Felski, "Women have been portrayed as victims of the ideology of consumerism, trapped in a web of objectified images which alienate them from their true identity. Any pleasure derived from fashion, cosmetics, women's magazines, or other distinctively feminized aspects of consumer culture has been read as merely another symptom of women's manipulation by institutionalized mechanisms of patriarchal control."[42] As Felski observes, some feminist scholars have rejected this "excessive puritanism," considering instead "the potential for active negotiation and recontextualization of meaning in the process of consumption."[43] The monstrous, devouring femme fatale was a figure invented by late-nineteenth-century male artists to cope with fears about women's emancipation, and the consuming woman is still regarded as excessive and threatening in a range of contexts. Cogan's textile works that represent women's consumption are not (in terms of intentionality) *about* mass consumption or consumer culture. They are not critiques of (mass) consumption, but rather illuminate the paradoxical and ambivalent relationship some women have with consumption and that which they consume, whether it be cocaine or cupcakes.

Writing in the early 1990s, feminist art historian Rosemary Betterton observed: "Chocolate, in particular, has taken on a symbolic cultural role with its connotations of richness and exclusivity and of wickedness and excess which gives it a moral as well as an edible dimension. Sweets and chocolate have become increasingly used as metaphors in art by women in the 1990s."[44] She adds that many women preferred chocolate as a mode of "safe sex"; a chemical found in chocolate—phenylethylamine—is also produced by the body during a sexual "high."[45] In the early 2000s, cupcakes replaced chocolate as the stereotypical go-to food for women who were perceived as eating their feelings or sublimating food for sex. Carrie and Miranda ate cupcakes on a bench while talking about their crushes in an episode of *Sex and the City*.[46] Cupcakes remain a kitschy, aestheticized, even fetishized, consumer product, aimed primarily at women. Cupcake boutiques have popped up in urban centers around the world—New York, London, Montreal, and elsewhere, although their popularity has ebbed somewhat in recent years. Borrowing display strategies from luxury boutiques, cupcake shops display their wares so as to aestheticize them as sensual, well-lit art objects for consumption. Cupcakes are usually colorful, and they are often given cute, humorous, or sensual names. The red velvet cupcake—evoking luxurious, opulent fabric—is a perennial favorite. And like cocaine, cupcakes have proved to be recession-proof.[47]

Unlike cupcakes, cocaine remains, in film and the news media, the powdery terrain of junkies and empty-eyed women who do not care about themselves or their bodies.[48] Kane Race, discussing the consumption of drugs in the context of pleasure and queer cultures, remarks: "As HIV enters a new, more manageable phase, illicit drugs appear to have taken up the slack in the public narrative of *just desserts* that has come to haunt gay life."[49] A similar argument could be made for women in the current sociopolitical climate. Susan Boyd reminds us that "all women, but especially poor women (both white women and women of color) and women who use illegal drugs, are regulated."[50] Thus to consume cocaine and cupcakes—both of which are gendered and classed[51]—is to embrace decadence in the everyday, the here and now.

Living for the moment was a particularly decadent philosophy in the late nineteenth century. As Elaine Showalter has commented, since "traditional consolations" such as nature, religion, and love were increasingly regarded as meaningless by decadent artists, "the only solution was to live in the experience of the moment."[52] Walter Pater articulated this Aesthetic (and decadent) philosophy in the famous Conclusion to *Studies in the History of the Renaissance* (1873) when he wrote:

> To burn always with this hard gem-like flame, to maintain this ecstasy, is success in life. Failure is to form habits; for habit is relative to a stereotyped world; meantime it is only the roughness of the eye that makes any two persons, things, situations, seem alike. While all melts under our feet, we may well catch at any exquisite passion, or any contribution to knowledge that seems, by a lifted horizon, to set the spirit free for a moment, or any stirring of the senses, strange dyes, strange flowers, and curious odours, or work of the artist's hands, or the face of one's friend. . . . With this sense of the splendour of our experience and of its awful brevity, gathering all we are into one desperate effort to see and touch, we shall hardly have time to make theories about the things we see and touch. What we have to do is to be for ever curiously testing new opinions and courting new impressions.[53]

He added: "The theory, or idea, or system, which requires of us the sacrifice of any part of this experience, in consideration of some interest into which we cannot enter, or some abstract morality we have not identified with ourselves, or what is only conventional, has no real claim upon us."[54] This philosophy, inevitably, was violently rejected by some as immoral and hedonistic, while it also found its disciples, such as Wilde and other aesthetes, who saw in Pater's book a celebration of homoerotic relationships. If we consider Pater's philosophy from a feminist perspective, his statement that "some abstract morality we have not identified with ourselves, or what is only conventional, has no real claim upon us" opens space for women to push against gendered ideologies related to consumption, pleasure, roles, behaviors, and lived experiences.

To represent the consumption of cocaine and cupcakes in a textile work of art is to align decadence with craft in a way that can only be called subversive. In works such as Cogan's *Bittersweet Obsession*, women are portrayed consuming both cupcakes and cocaine in ironically retro pastel textiles made out of fabrics that had previously been used in traditionally "feminine" and domestic contexts. According to neuroscientists and diet gurus, sugar attaches to the same part of the brain as narcotics, increasing serotonin, thus resulting in pleasure or respite from pain. Pleasure, then, would seem to be central to Cogan's cocaine/cupcake works.[55] In *Revisioning Women and Drug Use: Gender, Power and the Body* (2007), Elizabeth Ettore suggests that pleasure is part of female drug users' experiences, which may seem obvious. However, she points out that many sociologists have ignored this fact, and she proposes that this may in part be because women's drug use is still stigmatized and therefore it is either "not acceptable" or "confusing" to consider pleasure in the drugs field.[56] Pleasure is central in the following discussion, and it will continue to be a thread woven throughout the rest of the book.[57] According to Kane Race, in the context of illicit drugs, "Pointing to pleasure can function as a claim on understanding, an insistence on agency, and a sort of challenge."[58] As I discuss at the end of this chapter, pleasure and pain—or "pleasurable pain" to use Claire Bishop's phrase—has, since at least the early nineteenth century, been considered in relation to addictive substances.[59] Cogan, in pointing to the "bittersweetness" of pleasure, does not shy away from its paradoxes and risks.

It is significant that in her title Cogan deliberately uses the term "obsession" rather than the word "addiction." Obsession has negative connotations, but nothing like the word addiction. By combining the consumption of cupcakes and cocaine, Cogan is pointing toward women's consumption and women's pleasure as fundamentally subversive and transgressive. Cupcakes are cute, sweet, and nonthreatening, but combined with cocaine, they take on a darker, more bittersweet, taste. The consuming woman, the devouring woman, the woman who seeks pleasure, is still something of an enigma, or sphinx (a favorite theme of *fin-de-siècle* decadent artists),[60] and is therefore worth considering, both in visual and lived culture. Cogan's cheeky juxtaposition of baked goods and illicit substances, consumed by women in light blue denim jeans, flies in the face of historical representations of grotesque fat women and unhinged female drug addicts. There is humor here, surely, but there is also an opening for new ways to represent, theorize, and imagine women who desire pleasure, and who seek it out through both drugs and cupcakes.

Cogan and Waltener are not, unsurprisingly, the only contemporary artists concerned with baked goods. Montreal-based artist Shelley Miller has created a range of (ephemeral) luxury products, such as designer handbags, out of cake. According to Miller, her cake installations, such as *The Good Life Guide* (Figure 1.2), combine "the structure and composition of Dutch still life paintings with contemporary symbols of luxury and luxurious lifestyles. The seemingly recognizable and oft-overlooked formula of a still life painting is challenged by the fact that the objects in my work are sculpted out of edible cake and icing. Like the superfluous products I portray, cakes and sweets are highly desirable, often getting confused for necessity instead of an unnecessary luxury."[61] Miller notes that she is concerned with the themes of "indulgence and decadence," as well as with the "pleasure of looking," calling one of her photographs—which depicts a woman holding a small Louis Vuitton purse made out of cake—*Scopophilia*, which is part of her *Consumptuous* series (Figure 1.3).

Figure 1.2 Shelley Miller, *The Good Life Guide*, 2003. Courtesy of the artist.

Miller's work, historically loaded and theoretically sophisticated, may still provoke the age-old question from some corners: "But is it art?" Emily Holt's article "Flour Girls" appeared in the October 2013 issue of Vogue magazine. The article discusses entrepreneurs such as Amirah Kassem who are "trading fashion for frosting—and realizing just how closely those two worlds align."[62] Kassem launched a baking business called Flour Shop in 2012; she had previously been a general manager at the BLK DNM store in New York's SoHo area. Her creations do indeed mingle the worlds of baking and fashion. As Holt writes, "Friends of a Stella McCartney employee asked for a frosted re-creation of one of the designer's signature Falabella bags—though on Kassem's version, real slices of citrus fruit stood in for the spring 2011 print."[63] So, what distinguishes Miller's cakey handbags (Figures 1.3, 1.4 and 1.5) from Kassem's baked designs? Is it as simple as the former is art and the latter is popular culture? Or, put another way, does Miller's work *only* critique the consumption of luxury goods, while Kassem's work *only* celebrates

Figure 1.3 Shelley Miller, *Consumptuous*, 2006. Galerie Articule, Montreal. Courtesy of the artist.

Figure 1.4 Shelley Miller, *Eye Want You (LV) #1*, 2003. Courtesy of the artist.

Figure 1.5 Shelley Miller, *Eye Want You (LV)*, 2003. Installation view. Courtesy of the artist.

it? I would suggest that it is not that simple. As Claire Bishop has persuasively written in the context of participatory art, "We need to recognise art as a form of experimental activity overlapping with the world, whose negativity may lend support towards a political project (without bearing the sole responsibility for devising and implementing it), and—more radically—we need to support the progressive transformation of existing institutions through the transversal encroachment of ideas whose boldness is related to (and at times greater than) that of artistic imagination."[64] In other words, art and life inevitably overlap, but Bishop is also quick to remind us that art demands rigorous art criticism, and that despite a producer's intentionality, the critic—or art historian—must evaluate the work not only according to aesthetics, but also in terms of the ways in which the work "might offend or trouble its audience."[65] When this category of art is rejected, Bishop argues, "There is no space for perversity, paradox and negation."[66] As Bishop remarks: "By contrast, I would argue that unease, discomfort or frustration—along with fear, contradiction, exhilaration and absurdity—can be crucial to any work's impact." As should be apparent by now, although Cogan's textile works are not participatory or collaborative in the way that Waltener's *Sweet Nothings* was, Bishop's approach to contemporary art generally is highly useful for what she would call an "ethical" approach to *Bittersweet Obsession* and other works that represent the consumption of cupcakes and cocaine.

Many of Miller's sugar works *are* collaborative and participatory. Indeed, the performative component of works such as *The Good Life Guide* (a yellow sports car and golf shoes made out of cake) is the consumption—or partial consumption—of the shoes, poker pieces, and luxury handbags. The eating is only part of the artwork, and only part of the point. Likewise, Kessam's cakes—such as the Stella McCartney bag—are made to be consumed not only orally, but also visually. There is also, I would suggest, a haptic component, even an uncanny one. The sensation of looking at a cake—whether it was made by Miller or Kessam—and believing it to be a handbag made out of metal and high-end leather, followed by the experience of coming closer and realizing that what your eyes first read as leather is in fact icing, exemplifies an uncanny moment of ambivalence

Plate 1 Judy Chicago (American, born 1939). *The Dinner Party*, 1974–79. Ceramic, porcelain, textile, 576 × 576 in. (1463 × 1463 cm). Brooklyn Museum, Gift of The Elizabeth A. Sackler Foundation, 2002.10. © Judy Chicago.

Plate 2 Orly Cogan, *Bittersweet Obsession*, 2008. Vintage fabric, stitching, appliqué, paint. 127 × 127 cm. Museum of Art and Design, New York. Courtesy of the artist.

Plate 3 Orly Cogan, *Mirror, Mirror*, 2006. Hand-stitched embroidery, paint, and crochet on vintage linen, 19 × 24 in. Courtesy of the artist.

Plate 4 Orly Cogan, *Confections*, 2006. Courtesy of the artist.

Plate 5 Nava Lubelski, *Clumsy*, 2007. Collection of the artist. Copyright Nava Lubelski.

Plate 6 Shary Boyle, *To Colonize the Moon*, 2008. Porcelain, china paint, luster, diamond, mirror. 25 × 29 × 40 cm. Art Gallery of Ontario, Toronto. Photo by Rafael Goldchain.

Plate 7 Mickalene Thomas, *Are You That Someone?*, 2010. Rhinestones, acrylic, enamel on wood panel. © Mickalene Thomas. Courtesy of Mickalene Thomas, Lehmann Maupin, New York and Hong Kong, and Artists Rights Society (ARS), New York.

Plate 8 Mickalene Thomas, *I Learned the Hard Way*, 2010. Rhinestones, acrylic, enamel on wood panel, 120 × 96 in. © Mickalene Thomas. Courtesy of Mickalene Thomas, Susanne Veilmetter Los Angeles Projects, Los Angeles and Artists Rights Society (ARS), New York.

Plate 9 Shary Boyle, *Ouroboros*, 2006. Porcelain, enamel, luster, 16 × 26 × 18 cm. Collection of the artist.

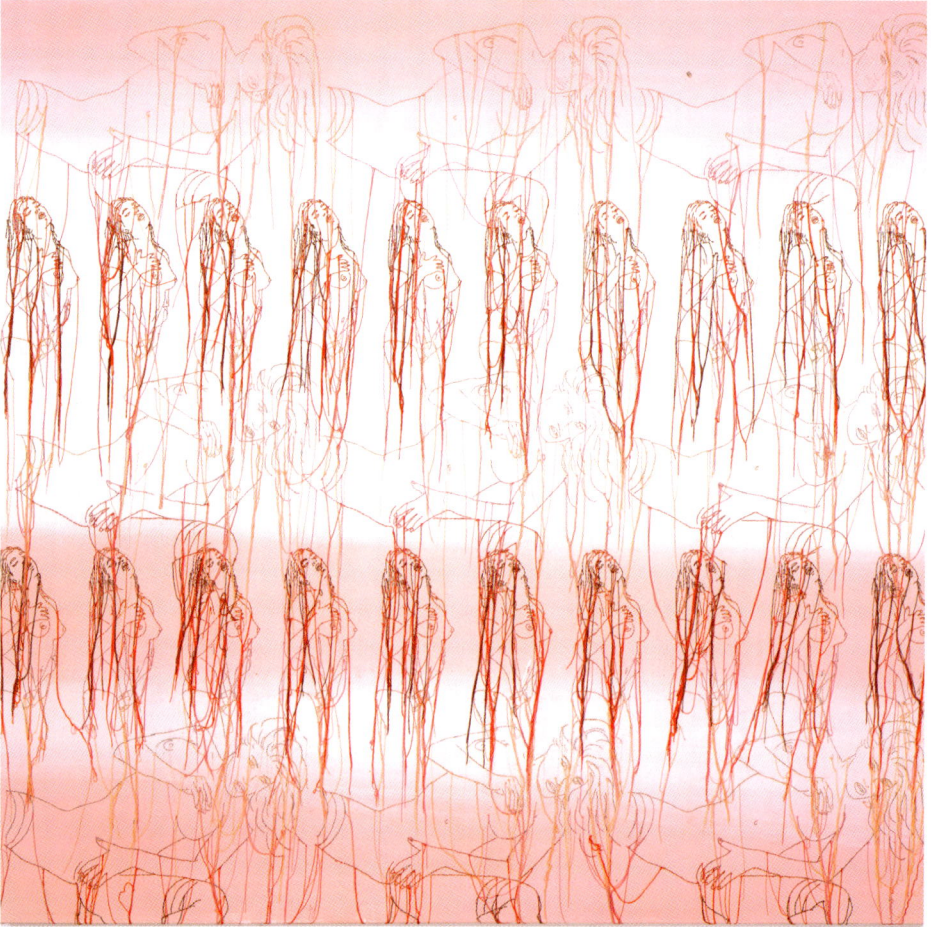

Plate 10 Ghada Amer, *Pink*, 2000. Acrylic, embroidery, and gel medium on canvas, 48 × 50 in. (122 × 127 cm).

Plate 11 Ghada Amer, *Knotty But Nice*, 2005. Acrylic, embroidery, and gel medium on canvas, 108 × 144 in. (274.3 × 365.8 cm).

Plate 12 Allyson Mitchell, detail from exhibition of *Ladies Sasquatch*, 2010. Found textiles, wood, Styrofoam, plastic, glass, fiberglass, and metal. McMaster Museum of Contemporary Art, Hamilton, Ontario. Photograph by Cat O'Neil. Courtesy of the artist.

Plate 13 Rozanne Hawksley, *Et ne non inducas (And Lead Us Not)*, 1987–89. Glove, 22 cm long. Courtesy of artist and Philip Hughes of Ruthin Craft Centre.

Plate 14 Rozanne Hawksley, *Libera me, domine, de morte aeterna (Deliver me, oh Lord, from eternal death)*, 1992. White glove with black sleeve with pearls, bones, and crucifix in black-lined box. Courtesy of artist and Philip Hughes of Ruthin Craft Centre.

Plate 15 Rozanne Hawksley, *Aimez-vous le big Mac?*, 2008. Glove. Courtesy of artist and Philip Hughes of Ruthin Craft Centre.

Plate 16 Rozanne Hawksley, *Queen of Spades*, 2008. White glove with black lace overlay, jewels and painted vellum playing cards. Courtesy of artist and Philip Hughes of Ruthin Craft Centre.

and recognition. Then, the physical sensation of cutting into a cake handbag, bringing it to your lips, and sinking your teeth into a Louis Vuitton purse made out of pound cake and icing engenders a transgression of boundaries fortified by beliefs about luxury and brand names. The pleasure caused by sugar rushing to the brain combines with not only the aesthetic pleasure of looking at luxury products, but also the transgressive pleasure of destroying luxury products. These multiple layers of pleasure would be experienced whether one was eating Miller's cakes or Kessam's cakes, which returns us to the question: but is it art? To my mind, Miller's cakes are conceptual art in that the objects are not the only component of the work; there is, as I have said, a performative component, but there is also a theoretical component that is related to a critique of luxury-obsession and consumption (by the few rather than the many). Miller has also noted that her sugar works are inextricably linked with waste, histories of slavery, and "cycles of guilt."[67]

Kassem's cakes, on the other hand, are very much part of that "obsession" with luxury, and indeed cater to some of the same clientele that would purchase the actual Stella McCartney handbag. This is not to denigrate Kassem's work, but simply to distinguish her project from Miller's. Holt notes at the end of her article: "Regardless of how seriously these women treat their baking ventures, at the end of the day their newfound passion is mostly about unadulterated fun."[68] I would suggest that one layer of Miller's radically decadent project is the notion that fun based in consumption, particularly the consumption of luxury goods, is always adulterated. Put another way, hers is a critical project that underscores the complexities, even risks, of pleasure. Her sugar works are founded in the knowledge that sugar, as a luxury, long had ties to the slave trade.[69] Miller's cakes speak to the fact that luxury products are always "tainted" by ethics and politics, labor and consumption.

The consuming woman as grotesque

In her book *Addiction to Perfection* (1982), psychoanalyst Marion Woodman writes: "Driven to do our best at school, on the job and in our relationships—in every corner of our lives—we try to make ourselves into works of art. Working so hard to create our own perfection we forget that we are human beings."[70] Woodman's book examines women's eating disorders from a Jungian feminist perspective. Her discussion of eating disorders as a self-destructive method of achieving an ostensible kind of corporeal perfection is worth considering in relation to Cogan's work. I propose that in these textiles Cogan represents the consumption of cocaine and cupcakes as acts that speak to a rejection of perfection. Further to this, Cogan represents young women consuming substances— drugs and baked goods—that have frequently been associated with the grotesque female body. Cogan's female subjects are clearly gendered and raced as white. In the visual culture of addiction, cocaine has often been raced as white and crack cocaine has usually been raced and classed as a drug consumed primarily by black males in lower-income areas in the United States.[71] The women in Cogan's textiles are young, white, slender, and clean. Susan Boyd, among others, has noted that typical physical signs associated with female drug use and addiction include unkempt hair, smeared mascara, and dirty clothes and skin.[72] Cogan therefore produces images that subvert the widely accepted, and expected, image of the female drug user and the female binger as physically grotesque and threatening to the social order. These works, however, are not straightforward celebrations of consumption, pleasure, and excess. Rather, as with many theorizations of the grotesque body, Cogan's textile works portray consumption, pleasure, and excess within a framework of ambivalence and paradox.

Nonetheless, I would argue that Cogan's artistic practice—the depiction of consumption using thread—is fundamentally transgressive in relation to historical and contemporary discourses related to female drug users and female bingers. Feminist craft scholar Rozsika Parker observed in her groundbreaking study *The Subversive Stitch* (1984): "That embroiderers do transform materials to produce sense—whole ranges of meanings—is invariably entirely overlooked. Instead embroidery and a stereotype of femininity have become collapsed into one another, characterised as mindless, decorative and delicate; like the icing on the cake, good to look at, adding taste and status, but devoid of significant content."[73] Cogan's textile works serve as evidence that contemporary feminist textile artists have moved beyond stereotypes of embroidery and femininity to produce subversive work that is full of meaning and "significant content," including women's consumption of illicit substances.

In Cogan's textile works, female subjects are portrayed snorting cocaine off what could be papers or textiles (Plate 2), or, more obviously, a mirror (Plate 3), an object that also appears in Shary Boyle's *To Colonize the Moon*, alongside a Medusa head (Plate 6). Charles Bernheimer describes the mirror as "perhaps the most widespread of decadent fetishes."[74] According to Cogan, "I mix subversion with flirtation, humor with power, and intimacy with frivolity. In the process I strive to inspire certain questions: What role do women play in society? Who do we want to be? What kind of relationships do we want to share? Who are our role models? In my work I hope to ask all of this within the context of constantly shifting boundaries that define our relationships and our identities."[75] These questions seem inadequate for a reading of Cogan's works through the critical framework of the grotesque. As previously noted, Cogan does not represent her female subjects as physically grotesque. But as Mary Russo reminds us, the grotesque "is only recognizable in relation to a norm and that exceeding the norm involves serious risk."[76] The female addict—or drug user—and the female binger—or consumer of baked goods—have often been portrayed and perceived as exceeding norms of femininity, and have thereby been framed as grotesque, excessive female bodies.

Film scholar Barbara Creed has remarked that "all human societies have a conception of the monstrous-feminine, of what it is about woman that is shocking, terrifying, horrific, abject."[77] It is my contention that both the female drug user and the female binger have been represented and imagined as the monstrous-feminine. Historically, male artists have depicted the female "excessive" drinker and the female drug user as grotesque, employing a range of aesthetic strategies. In British artist William Hogarth's famous engraving *Gin Lane* (1751), the central female figure is rendered grotesque by way of her physiognomy, bared breasts, and lack of attention to her falling infant. In Swiss artist Eugène Samuel Grasset's lithograph *Morphinomaniac* (1897), a beautiful woman with thick black hair and ivory skin is transformed into a "maniac" when she is portrayed with animalistic bared teeth, indicating physical withdrawal, and arthritic-looking hands that clench her thigh as she prepares to inject herself with morphine.[78] These two works serve to exemplify the body of work that I call the visual culture of addiction: imagery that has been produced and consumed as visual "evidence" that addiction is legible from the body.

In *Revisioning Women and Drug Use: Gender, Power and the Body* (2007), Elizabeth Ettorre notes that drug use, particularly women's drug use, is often pictured as "embodied deviance," and she alludes to the "scientific and lay claim that bodies of individuals classified as deviant are marked in some recognizable way."[79] It has long been believed, erroneously, that drug use and addiction can be read from physical "signs" on the body. By critically examining both visual representations of ostensibly addicted individuals and textual descriptions of addicted individuals that apparently support the belief that addiction is legible from visual evidence, it is possible to rigorously and effectively deconstruct that very belief.[80] Cogan's textile works, I would argue, do critical, feminist work within this discourse; this is in part what makes them radically decadent. The women in her textiles that represent the consumption of cocaine do not exhibit any corporeal "signs" of drug use or addiction, and it is crucial to emphasize again that drug use is not synonymous with or symptomatic of addiction. Works such as *Bittersweet Obsession* and *Mirror, Mirror* subvert the belief that the act of consuming illicit drugs—still a societal stigma—inevitably leaves traces (or "stigmata") on the body. In 1920, the New York City Narcotic Clinic released a report that included the following passage:

> We do not know who the addicts are, nor how many there are of them, either here or elsewhere in this country. Why? From opinions expressed, and from the literature on this subject, we have been led to believe that addiction was allocated with definite physical stigmata; pallor, emaciation, nervousness, apprehension, sniffing, needle puncture markings, and tattoo skin evidences; but in actual experience with hundreds of acknowledged drug addicts, persons actually seeking their drug, we find, like weather indications, all such signs failing.[81]

Nonetheless, the belief that drug use and addiction are legible from the body endures, as does the related belief that the bodies of the female drug user and female addict are discursively, if not physically, monstrous.[82] Ettorre remarks: "In the hierarchies of social values . . . women drug users remain outside the realm of the respectable and are more easily classified as dangerous, bad, risky or monstrous bodies."[83]

There is a related belief about the ostensible monstrosity of the woman who eats "excessively." According to Betterton, "Femininity and the consumption of food are intimately connected and, in women, fatness is taken to signify both loss of control and a failure of feminine identity."[84] In her essay "Body Horror? Food (and Sex and Death) in Women's Art," Betterton examines feminist artworks produced in the 1990s that highlight themes related to food and the female body. She sees these works as attempts "to explore our ambivalent fascinations with and fears of our own changing, consuming, and desiring corporeal being."[85] Significantly, she also links these feminist artworks with the grotesque female body.[86] Betterton argues that many feminist artists of the 1990s employed the theoretical and aesthetic apparatus of the abject—the transgression between inside and outside, and between self and other—to critique the misogyny of

Western culture and "its deep hostility to the female and maternal body." She argues, however, that "the 'monstrous-feminine' cannot simply be reclaimed for women, and its use in art remains a deeply ambivalent process."[87] Cogan's textile works that represent the consumption of cocaine and cupcakes depart from earlier feminist artworks that depict physically grotesque female bodies, in that she portrays her female subjects not as physically grotesque or monstrous, but rather as attractive and healthy-looking, despite their (ostensible) excesses.

Betterton quotes Susan Bordo's important work on women's eating disorders in her essay on food in feminist art. Bordo observes: "Many of us may find our lives vacillating between a daytime rigidly ruled by the 'performance principle' while our nights and weekends capitulate to an unconscious 'letting go' (food, shopping, liquor, and other addictive drugs). In this way, the central contradiction of the system inscribes itself on our bodies, and bulimia emerges as a characteristic modern personality construction."[88] Interestingly, Betterton suggests that food is gendered as feminine, and she implies that alcohol (and we might, surmise, other addictive substances) are gendered as masculine in Western culture. By juxtaposing the consumption of cupcakes and cocaine in her textile works, Cogan subverts this dichotomy, exposing the fact that women consume both drugs and baked goods for pleasure. Yet, this pleasure is not without consequences, and it is sometimes characterized by shame and remorse. Indeed, Cogan's title *Bittersweet Obsession* points to both pleasure and ambivalence, and to the push-pull of desire and repulsion that is often noted in discussions of women's relationship with food. As Betterton remarks, "Bulimics . . . describe the intense pleasures they derive from eating, especially food associated with indulgence and excess like ice-cream, chocolate or junk food. . . . But at the same time, feelings of guilt, depression and self-loathing which accompany the bulimic experience would suggest that it represents an attempt to deal with contradictory nexus of repressions and desires around the female body."[89] None of Cogan's textile works are explicitly about the experience of bulimia, but with titles such as *Bittersweet Obsession* and *Gorging*, the viewer is guided toward interpretations of her works that are informed by contradictory ideas regarding women, food, and "excess."

Mary Russo notes that "like other categories of abjections which have historically been related to the grotesque, fatness and bodily excess of various kinds are most often thought of in passive, individual, or merely descriptive terms and, indeed . . . fat women in the United States particularly, are repositories of shame and repressed desire."[90] Significantly, Cogan does not depict her female subjects as fat, thus complicating the vision of the woman who binges or "gorges" on baked goods. Her women are not extremely thin, nor are they noticeably overweight. They are, however, usually naked, except for socks. For instance, in one of Cogan's works entitled *Cupcake Girl* (Figure 1.1), a woman is depicted eating what appear to be two chocolate cupcakes. Betterton observes that "chocolate, in particular, has taken on a symbolic cultural role with its connotations of richness and exclusivity and of wickedness and excess which gives it a moral as well as an edible dimension."[91] In Cogan's *Cupcake Girl*, the woman is represented in a seated position, and she wears striped, colorful socks. The vintage linen has a worked border of embroidered flowers that surround the female figure. Cogan's aesthetic strategy of representing her female subjects naked, except for socks, is ambiguous. It might be intended for humorous effect.[92] Another possible interpretation is that these textiles allude to the practice described in some texts on eating disorders and "food addiction," namely, the practice of women returning home after work and immediately beginning to consume junk food.[93] The fact that the female subjects in these works are naked except for socks suggests that they are in the privacy of their own homes and that they have recently undressed, but have begun eating before putting on other—perhaps more comfortable—clothes. In Cogan's textile works, the consumption of baked goods is portrayed as a solitary activity, which may or may not indicate that shame is involved.

As previously noted, although there are multiple figures represented in *Bittersweet Obsession*, the consumption of cupcakes and that of cocaine are both portrayed as solitary activities. Two women (both are naked; one wears socks) eat cupcakes in the lower register; two clothed women snort cocaine in the upper section; and a woman cuts into a cake decorated with strawberries in the center. The two women consuming cocaine recall the woman in *Mirror, Mirror* in that all three female subjects are wearing blue jeans and t-shirts (Plate 3). As I have been arguing, drug use, baking, and crafting can all be engaged in as ways of seeking community or communion with other human beings. But all three can also be done alone. By representing her female subjects as solitary, Cogan seems to suggest that the consumption of cupcakes and cocaine are ambivalent acts predicated upon both the desire for pleasure and (possibly) feelings of shame. Nonetheless, Cogan's representations of women consuming drugs and baked goods do not frame the female subjects as physically or morally monstrous. They are desiring and consuming subjects, and thus subjects with, arguably, power and a kind of freedom.[94]

Helen Keane remarks that "the (assumed) connection between eating habits and body size and shape adds further levels of meaning to food consumption. In the contemporary West, slenderness is read not only as physically attractive and healthy, but as a sign of moral rectitude; evidence of self-control, self-reliance, and industriousness. The fat body, in turn, connotes greed, laziness, and lack of care for the self."[95] Despite pointing to ambivalence and feelings of both attraction and repulsion to drugs and baked goods (primarily through her titles), Cogan subverts expectations related to the ostensible legibility of drug use and "excessive" food consumption from the body. These textiles, then, not only disturb the Western belief that female drug users and women who eat "to excess" are (symbolically) grotesque and monstrous, but also destabilize the long-standing belief that both drug use and "excessive" consumption of specific foods (particularly baked goods) are legible from physical evidence on the (female) body. Cogan's textile works are therefore, paradoxically, "grotesque" in the feminist sense: they speak of ambivalence, contradiction, attraction, and repulsion; they are sites of resistance; and they are fundamentally subversive in that they destabilize discourses related to women and expectations of perfection.

Conclusion

In her book *From Witches to Crack Moms: Women, Drug Law, and Policy*, Susan C. Boyd observes that "drug laws are supported by myths and ideologies that intensify the regulation of women. Ideology is significant in relation to understanding the thinking that is involved in the moral regulation and disciplining of women who use illegal drugs."[96] Boyd goes on to argue that "women who use illegal drugs have long been constructed as the 'Other', who is outside the norms of proper moral and gendered female behavior. Traditional discourse about the female illegal drug user is embedded with gendered power relations."[97] Cogan's textiles are, in light of facts regarding policy, drug law, addiction discourse, and deviance models of illicit drug users, extremely radical, depicting as they do explicit acts of cocaine consumption (an illegal act), juxtaposed with women eating cupcakes. The works might be said to be tongue-in-cheek representations of women consuming for pleasure; whether these are portraits of Cogan and/or friends or not, they are radical works that fly in the face of gendered drug laws, punitive drug policy, and discourses revolving around the ostensible deviancy (and immorality) of illicit drug users. Cogan acknowledges with her titles that seeking pleasure via drugs and baked goods may not be without affective consequences, but her women are not monstrous, grotesque, criminal, or decaying. These women subvert the widely accepted (and expected) image of the "deviant" female drug user. In *The Subversive Stitch*, Parker states: "For women today, the contradictory and complex history of embroidery is important because it reveals that definitions of sexual difference, and the definitions of art and artist so weighted against women, are not fixed. They have shifted over the centuries, and they can be transformed in the future."[98] Feminist artists working with textiles have employed a range of strategies to enact subversion. In Cogan's works that represent women consuming both cocaine and cupcakes, she is subverting a range of ideologies related to women's consumption and to specific substances, including baked goods and illicit drugs. As Cogan comments in a video created for the VOLTA 9 art show in Basel in 2013, "Many of my pieces are a celebration of indulgence in a lot of ways."[99] Hers is not a straightforward celebration, however. It is complicated by her titles, which not only allude to the physical and affective realities of consuming drugs and baked goods, but also evoke the still-circulating discourses that revolve around the body of the consuming woman. Scholars such as Rosemary Betterton, Barbara Creed, and Mary Russo have theorized the consuming, monstrous, grotesque woman. Cogan's consuming women are not depicted as monstrous or grotesque, and in this way, her stitches are subversive. By juxtaposing cocaine and cupcakes, she unveils the open secret that women consume for pleasure, despite the risks, and that whether illicit or licit, women will get their hands on what they want.

In *Artificial Hells*, Bishop asserts that one of art's roles is to elicit "perverse, disturbing and pleasurable experiences that enlarge our capacity to imagine the world and our relations anew."[100] Even more importantly for my purposes here, Bishop reminds us that "the most urgent forms of artistic practice today stem from a necessity to rethink the connections between the individual and collective along these lines of painful pleasure— rather than conforming to a self-suppressing sense of social obligation."[101] There are echoes of Pater's philosophy in this statement. Furthermore, pleasure is central to all three of the experiences that I have been concerned with in this chapter: crafting and the consumption of baked goods and illicit drugs. Pleasure, of course, is a complex concept.[102] To Cogan's credit, she does not reduce the experience of consuming cupcakes and cocaine to the simplistic motive of pleasure, alluding instead to the ambivalent relationship that many—though not all—women have with food and/or drugs, not only with her titles, such as *Bittersweet Obsession*, but also through the ways that she represents her female subjects. We may note, for instance, that none of them are smiling.

Although Cogan may be "celebrating indulgence" in her cocaine and cupcake works, the textiles cannot be said to be simplistic depictions of consumption, and in highlighting the complexity of consumption, the paradoxes, the ambivalence, and even the risks, Cogan's textile art begins to unstitch over one hundred years of addiction discourse that has framed women drug users as deviant and monstrous. As Rosemary Betterton has observed, "Food offers a way of exploring the pleasures and dangers of the body's limits in ways which are particularly relevant for women, both because food is culturally gendered as feminine and because it provides means of discovering the contradictory, ambivalent and often unresolved feelings relating to feminine identity."[103] Cogan's work proposes that both food *and* drugs, as radically decadent subjects, can interrogate gendered ideologies related to women, female bodies, excess, and art.

Notes

1 For more on this, see Julia Skelly, "The Paradox of Excess: Oscar Wilde, Caricature, and Consumption," in Skelly (ed.), *The Uses of Excess in Visual and Material Culture, 1600-2010*, 137–60. See also Elizabeth K. Menon, "Decadent Addictions: Tobacco, Alcohol, Popular Imagery, and Café Culture in France," in Dixon (ed.), with the assistance of Gabriel P. Weisberg, *In Sickness and in Health: Disease as Metaphor in Art and Popular Wisdom*, 101–24.

2 Quoted in Elaine Showalter, *Sexual Anarchy: Gender and Culture at the Fin de Siècle* (New York: Viking, 1990), 170.

3 "A race which is regularly addicted, even without excess, to narcotics and stimulants in any form (such as fermented alcoholic drinks, tobacco, opium, hashish, arsenic) . . . begets degenerate descendants who, if they remain exposed to the same influences, rapidly descend to the lowest degrees of degeneracy, to idiocy, to dwarfishness, etc." Max Nordau, *Degeneration* (1892; Lincoln and London: University of Nebraska Press, 2006), 34. Heidi Brevik-Zender has discussed Nordau's views on "decadent" interiors. Heidi Brevik-Zender, "Decadent Decors and Torturous Textiles: Fatal Fashions and Interior Design in the Fin-de-Siècle Novels of Rachilde," in John Potvin and Alla Myzelev (eds), *Fashion, Interior Design and the Contours of Modern Identity* (Farnham and Burlington, VT: Ashgate, 2010), 105–23.

4 As discussed in the Introduction, feminist scholars Bridget Elliott and Jasmine Rault have examined the politics and aesthetics of decadence in terms of specific female artists and designers. This chapter contributes to the feminist literature that discusses decadence in the context of feminist approaches to both art and lived experience. My investigation departs from Elliott's and Rault's scholarship in that it focuses on contemporary artists and issues related to consumption, primarily the consumption of baked goods and illicit drugs. See Elliott, "Housing the Work," 176–91; Bridget Elliott, "Performing the Picture or Painting the Other: Romaine Brooks, Gluck and the Question of Decadence in 1923," in Katy Deepwell (ed.), *Women Artists and Modernism* (Manchester and New York: Manchester University Press, 1998), 70–82; Jasmine Rault, *Eileen Gray and the Design of Sapphic Modernity: Staying In* (Farnham and Burlington: Ashgate, 2011).

5 "The Politics of Craft: A Roundtable," in Glenn Adamson (ed.), *The Craft Reader* (Oxford and New York: Berg, 2010), 621.

6 Jefferies, "Contemporary Textiles," 46.

7 Maria Elena Buszek, "Introduction: The Ordinary Made Extra/Ordinary," in Buszek (ed.), *Extra/Ordinary: Craft and Contemporary Art*, 1.

8 Claire Bishop, *Artificial Hells: Participatory Art and the Politics of Spectatorship* (London and New York: Verso, 2012), 1.

9 "Needlework has a revolutionary past. It was used as a symbol of dissent by William Morris—one of the founders of the Arts and Crafts Movement—in his protest against industrial production. So that his work could continue to be produced by hand, Morris defied industrialists to support the Royal School of Needlework and single-handedly revitalized the art of tapestry-weaving in Britain. A similar rebellion was sparked a century later when feminist artists incorporated embroidery into their artwork. They challenged the distinction between art and craft that separated fibre art and fine art." Bradley Quinn, "Textiles at the Cutting Edge," in Monem (ed.), *Contemporary Textiles: The Fabric of Fine Art*, 15. See also Anthea Callen, *Women in the Arts and Crafts Movement, 1870-1914* (London: Astragal Books, 1980).

10 For more on the relationship between women, shame, and addictive substances, see Julia Skelly, *Wasted Looks: Addiction and British Visual Culture, 1751-1919* (Farnham, UK, and Burlington, VT: Ashgate, 2014), especially Chapter 1.

11 Shu Hung and Joseph Magliaro (eds), *By Hand: The Use of Craft in Contemporary Art* (New York: Princeton Architectural Press, 2007), 14.

12 "Shane Waltener," in Shu Hung and Joseph Magliaro (eds), *By Hand: The Use of Craft in Contemporary Art* (New York: Princeton Architectural Press, 2007), 160.

13 Jefferies, "Loving Attention," 233.

14 See Lisa Tickner, "Banners and Banner-Making," in Vanessa R. Schwartz and Jeannene M. Przyblyski (eds), *The Nineteenth-Century Visual Culture Reader* (New York and London: Routledge, 2004), 341–48; Julia Skelly, "Object Lessons: The Social Life of Temperance Banners," *Textile: The Journal of Cloth and Culture* 14, no. 3 (2016): 268–93.

15 See Nicolas Bourriaud, *Relational Aesthetics* (Paris: Le Presses due reel, 1998; translated 2002).

16 Quinn, "Textiles at the Cutting Edge," 15.

17 Jefferies, "Loving Attention," 233.

18 Ibid., 234.

19 Ibid., 233.

20 Ibid.

21 For photographs of Waltener's *Sweet Nothings*, see Jefferies, "Loving Attention."

22 Bishop, *Artificial Hells*, 5.

23 Email exchange between Shane Waltener and Janis Jefferies. Quoted in Jefferies, "Loving Attention," 234.

24 Quoted in Betterton, "Body Horror?" 149. See Lorraine Gamman and Merja Makinen, *Female Fetishism: A New Look* (London: Lawrence & Wishart, 1994), 167. Betterton writes: "Fetishism, they argue, is culturally gendered and, for women, focuses primarily on food as its object. Their work offers an important revision of the model of (passive) female sexuality within orthodox psychoanalytic accounts and reconstitutes women as active agents of their own desires" (149). For further discussion, see Helen Keane, "Disorders of Eating and the Healthy Diet: How to Eat Well," in *What's Wrong with Addiction?* (New York: New York University Press, 2002), 117.

25 Elizabeth A. Sackler Center for Feminist Art: Feminist Art Base, Brooklyn Museum, https://www.brooklynmuseum.org/eascfa/feminist_art_base/gallery/orlycogan.php?i=456 (last accessed November 27, 2013).

26 Quoted in Betterton, "Body Horror?" 157.

27 Email exchange between Cogan and author, November 27, 2013.

28 Philippe Jullian, *Dreamers of Decadence: Symbolist Painters of the 1890s*, trans. Robert Baldick (New York: Praeger Publishers, 1971), 244.

29 *Pricked: Extreme Embroidery* (New York: Museum of Arts and Design, 2007), 76.

30 Jefferies, "Contemporary Textiles," 44n21.

31 Dennis Stevens, "Validity Is in the Eye of the Beholder: Mapping Craft Communities of Practice," in Buszek (ed.), *Extra/Ordinary: Craft and Contemporary Art*, 46.

32 Kane Race, *Pleasure Consuming Medicine: The Queer Politics of Drugs* (Durham and London: Duke University Press, 2009), 20.

33 Ibid.

34 Ibid., 23.

35 Tom Yardley, *Why We Take Drugs: Seeking Excess and Communion in the Modern World* (New York and London: Routledge, 2012), 7.

36 Ibid., 74.

37 Ibid., 93.

38 See Susan C. Boyd, *From Witches to Crack Moms: Women, Drug Law, and Policy* (Durham, NC: Carolina Academic Press, 2004); Elizabeth Ettorre, *Revisioning Women and Drug Use: Gender, Power and the Body* (New York: Palgrave Macmillan, 2007).

39 For a discussion that examines heroin use by thirty white middle- and upper-class women as a mode of resistance against restrictive gender and class expectations, see Jennifer Friedman and Marisa Alicea, "Women and Heroin: The Path of Resistance and its Consequences," *Gender and Society* 9, no. 4 (August 1995): 432–49.

40 Hung and Magliaro, *By Hand*, 14.

41 Kirsty Robertson, "Rebellious Doilies and Subversive Stitches: Writing a Craftivist History," in Buszek (ed.), *Extra/Ordinary: Craft and Contemporary Art*, 187.

42 Rita Felski, *The Gender of Modernity* (Cambridge, MA, and London: Harvard University Press, 1995), 63.

43 Ibid.

44 Betterton, "Body Horror?" 157.

45 Ibid., 156.

46 For a discussion of career women as consumers in the urban landscape, see Leslie Kern, *Sex and the Revitalized City: Gender, Condominium Development, and Urban Citizenship* (Vancouver and Toronto: University of British Columbia Press, 2010), especially Chapters 2 and 5.

47 Ole Bjerg, "Drug Addiction and Capitalism: Too Close to the Body," *Body & Society* 14, no. 2 (June 2008): 1–22.

48 See Susan C. Boyd, *Hooked: Drug War Films in Britain, Canada, and the United States* (Toronto: University of Toronto Press, 2008).

49 Race, *Pleasure Consuming Medicine*, 140. Emphasis added.

50 Boyd, *From Witches to Crack Moms*, xvii.

51 In popular culture and the media, cocaine is often—though not always—aligned with success and money, while crack cocaine has often been aligned with African American and lower-economic status individuals. See Jimmie L. Reeves and Richard Campbell, *Cracked Coverage: Television News, the Anti-Cocaine Crusade, and the Reagan Legacy* (Durham, NC, and London: Duke University Press, 1994).

52 Showalter, *Sexual Anarchy*, 169.

53 Walter Pater, *Studies in the History of the Renaissance* (1873; Oxford: Oxford University Press, 2010), 120.

54 Ibid.

55 See P. O'Malley and M. Valverde, "Pleasure, Freedom and Drugs: The Uses of 'Pleasure' in Liberal Governance of Drug and Alcohol Consumption," *Sociology* 38, 1 (2004): 25–42.

56 Ettorre, *Revisioning Women and Drug Use*, 44.

57 See Craig Reinarman, "Policing Pleasure: Food, Drugs, and the Politics of Ingestion," *Gastronomica: The Journal of Food and Culture* 7, no. 3 (Summer 2007): 53–61.

58 Race, *Pleasure Consuming Medicine*, ix.

59 Barry Milligan, *Pleasures and Pains: Opium and the Orient in Nineteenth-Century British Culture* (Charlottesville and London: University Press of Virginia, 1995).

60 Jullian, *Dreamers of Decadence*, 65. See also Elizabeth Wilson, *The Sphinx in the City: Urban Life, the Control of Disorder, and Women* (London: Virago Press, 1991).

61 Quoted on Shelley Miller's official website. http://www.shelleymillerstudio.com/(last accessed November 26, 2013).

62 Emily Holt, "Flour Girls," *Vogue* (October 2013): 224.

63 Ibid.

64 Bishop, *Artificial Hells*, 284.

65 Ibid., 25.

66 Ibid., 40.

67 In conversation with author, September 14, 2015.

68 Holt, "Flour Girls," 228.

69 See Kay Dian Kriz, *Slavery, Sugar, and the Culture of Refinement: Picturing the British West Indies, 1700-1840* (New Haven: Yale University Press, 2008).

70 Marion Woodman, *Addiction to Perfection: The Still Unravished Bride* (Toronto: Inner City Books, 1982), 10.

71 See Boyd, *Hooked*.

72 Ibid., 90.

73 Rozsika Parker, *The Subversive Stitch: Embroidery and the Making of the Feminine* (1984; London and New York: I. B. Tauris, 2010), 6.

74 Charles Bernheimer, "Fetishism and Decadence: Salome's Severed Heads," in Emily Apter and William Pketz (eds), *Fetishism as Cultural Discourse* (Ithaca and London: Cornell University Press, 1993), 82.

75 Quoted in *Pricked*, 76.

76 Mary Russo, *The Female Grotesque: Risk, Excess and Modernity* (New York and London: Routledge, 1994), 10.

77 Barbara Creed, *The Monstrous-Feminine: Film, Feminism, Psychoanalysis* (New York and London: Routledge, 1993), 1.

78 For more on this work, see Skelly, *Wasted Looks*, 139.

79 Ettorre, *Revisioning Women and Drug Use*, 29.

80 For more on this, see Skelly, *Wasted Looks*.

81 Quoted in Charles E. Terry and Mildred Pellens, *The Opium Problem* (New York: The Committee on Drug Addictions in Collaboration with the Bureau of Social Hygiene, 1928), 33.

82 See Boyd, *Hooked*.

83 Ettorre, *Revisioning Women and Drug Use*, 59.

84 Betterton, "Body Horror?" 131.

85 Ibid., 132.

86 Ibid., 137.

87 Ibid., 138.

88 Quoted in ibid., 131.

89 Ibid., 151.

90 Russo, *The Female Grotesque*, 24.

91 Betterton, "Body Horror?" 157.

92 *I Want Candy: The Sweet Stuff in American Art* (Yonkers, NY: Hudson River Museum, 2007), 23.

93 Keane, *What's Wrong with Addiction?* 118.

94 See O'Malley and Valverde, "Pleasure, Freedom and Drugs." See also Tammy L. Anderson, "Dimensions of Women's Power in the Illicit Drug Economy," *Theoretical Criminology* 9, no. 4 (2005): 371–400.

95 Ibid., 111.

96 Boyd, *From Witches to Crack Moms*, 7.

97 Ibid., 16.

98 Parker, *The Subversive Stitch*, 215.

99 Orly Cogan, video, VOLTA 9, Basel 2013 (www.gallerylog.com), http://vimeo.com/67696274.

100 Bishop, *Artificial Hells*, 248.

101 Ibid., 39.

102 See Dan W. Brock, "Can Pleasure Be Bad for You?" *The Hastings Center Report* 13, no. 4 (August 1983): 30–34. Brock, a philosopher, asks two pointed questions at the outset of his essay: "A significant source of the support for continuing strong legal prohibition on the use of drugs merely for pleasure is the common attitude that such use is bad. Is there any sound basis for disapproving of the pleasure that is produced by drug use, and if so what can it be? And more specifically, is there any sound basis for disapproving of the use of drugs for pleasure itself rather than because of other consequences that taking drugs has, or may have?" (30).

103 Betterton, "Body Horror?" 160.

2

PLEASURE CRAFT: NAVA LUBELSKI, MICKALENE THOMAS, AND SHARY BOYLE

Pleasure and craft

Picking up on one of the threads of Chapter 1, this chapter considers the concepts of pleasure and decadence as analytical frameworks for contemporary feminist art that pushes against gendered beliefs about women's consumption. A number of contemporary feminist artists—such as Orly Cogan (Plate 2) and Nava Lubelski (Plate 5), among others—have produced works that represent or allude to women consuming food and/ or addictive substances.[1] Both Cogan and Lubelski have produced these kinds of works using textiles historically associated with domestic (or "feminine") activities in the kitchen. These artists' transformations of domestic textiles into "subversive stitches," to quote Rozsika Parker, is, I argue, an important instance of reinvention in contemporary feminist textile art. Further to this, works by Cogan and Lubelski are concerned with *pleasure*, in terms of both subject matter and the materials chosen.

This chapter also examines works by Brooklyn-based artist Mickalene Thomas and Canadian artist Shary Boyle through the lens of radical decadence, considering their representations of black and white women, respectively, in the context of visual and other pleasures. In employing materials traditionally associated with craft—namely, fiber, rhinestones, and ceramics—these four artists have deliberately "failed" in relation to the art/craft hierarchy, as described and critiqued by craft scholars such as Elissa Auther, according to which (amateur, feminine) "craft" has been denigrated in relation to (masculine) "art." As Auther elaborates:

> Throughout the twentieth century the basic assumptions about craft's inadequacies vis-à-vis fine art were maintained and reinforced explicitly through classification and implicitly through critical categories such as the decorative, among others. The critical power of this term when used negatively, that is, when a work of art is characterized as "merely decorative," was rooted in part in the hierarchical relation of art to craft. . . . In [Clement] Greenberg's criticism about modern art, the decorative was associated with superficial surface embellishment, skilled labor, derivativeness, and precision in a mechanical rather than "felt out" manner of working.[2]

This ostensible "superficial surface embellishment" is what has been deemed as "excessive" about craft. As I discuss later in this chapter, Mickalene Thomas in particular plays with the idea of certain materials being superficial, superfluous, and therefore excessive, by adding rhinestones to her paintings. It is evident from some art criticism that this kind of serious play with craft materials still causes unease in some viewers. Boyle too plays with materiality and excess, producing porcelain sculptures of monstrous women wearing elaborate gowns made out of dipped lace.

The intersecting issues of women's lives, labors, and failures are explicit throughout Joanna Frueh's article "Making a Mess: Women's Bane, Women's Pleasure." As she comments, "Within modernist discourse and modern life, the woman artist who 'makes a mess' has not experienced success equal to men's. This is because tidiness has been and remains a norm imposed by culture on women."[3] Frueh argues that "academic and art-world feminists have negated, screened, silenced, constrained, and marginalised women's pleasure—have barely begun to develop a feminist, female erotics—and have capitulated to pain."[4] Frueh suggests that women have often avoided or denied themselves pleasure because of shame. She also remarks that "social relevance is not necessarily aesthetic necessity, visual pleasure, or a much-needed radical vision of women's pleasure, as too many post-feminist 'hurts-so-good' artworks have demonstrated."[5] In her discussion of (visual) pleasure, Frueh focuses on feminist/women artists of the 1970s, such as performance artist Carolee Schneemann. In this chapter I want to argue that many feminist artists of the more recent past who are working with craft materials have explicitly engaged with pleasure: not only visual pleasure, but also the pleasure that comes from food and addictive substances such as cocaine and alcohol.[6] This pleasure is not without perils, however. Stains, hangovers, guilt, and shame are only some of the complicating factors that women can encounter when seeking pleasure. Frueh also highlights the dangers of "going mad" for brilliant women who have sought pleasure, noting that "madness is excessive."[7] I want to move away from the connection that has been made between women's pleasure and women's (ostensible) madness, focusing instead on the complicated pleasures of women living in the twenty-first century as illuminated by works by Orly Cogan, Nava Lubelski, Mickalene Thomas, and Shary Boyle.

In her 1996 study of contemporary installation art by women artists in Canada, Judith Mastai proposed that anorexia could function as a metaphor for this kind of three-dimensional artwork. Mastai was concerned with the impact of funding provided by the Canada Council to women artists, and she found that the "place of the body of the maker in the work seemed a major preoccupation for the artists whose work I investigated. And the image that occurred to me as a metaphor for this preoccupation was the anorexic body: starving in the presence of a controlled and controlling overabundance."[8] One of the artists whom Mastai discusses is Jana Sterbak, who is currently based in Montreal, Canada. Mastai considers in particular Sterbak's dress works from the late 1980s, including *I Want You To Feel the Way I Do* (1985) and her more well-known work, *Vanitas: Flesh Dress for an Albino Anorectic* (1987), which is a dress made out of raw flank steak. In photographs documenting the work, a thin white woman is shown wearing the garment. For Mastai, *Vanitas* "almost too perfectly illustrates the metaphor of the anorexic body—present through absence and therefore mourned."[9] Mastai comments close to the end of her essay:

> In Canada today, installation works are the predominant three-dimensional form of women's work supported by the institutions of art. It has been disturbing to investigate this phenomenon and to conclude that it may stand for a form of anorexic self-regulation. Even more disturbing is a further question: Is the representation of the disappearing, anorexic body a symptom of internalized mental regulation, learned by women as a result of their socio-political conditioning, or is it a representation of female desire, a representation of self-regulation, deprivation and disappearance as pleasure?[10]

The artists discussed in this chapter, working with particular forms of three-dimensional art—namely, textiles and ceramics, as well as paint and rhinestones—are not (re)presenting what could be read as the anorexic body, nor are they engaging with the kind of "pleasure" that may be derived from "self-regulation, deprivation and disappearance." Neither can the metaphor of anorexia be productively used to consider the critical work that these objects are doing. Rather, many feminist artists—not only those discussed in this chapter, but also Tracey Emin, Ghada Amer, Allyson Mitchell, and Rozanne Hawksley, whom I discuss in later chapters—are engaging with women's pleasure: visual pleasure, the pleasure of looking, the pleasure(s) of consumption, the pleasure of (forbidden) touch, and yes, the pleasures of (perceived) excess, even when these pleasures are often complicated and paradoxical.

Pleasure/failure/risk

Cogan and Lubelski, in producing works that portray "excessive" consuming women—through figurative representation as in Cogan's textiles (Figures 2.1 and 2.2) or in absentia through traces in the form of stains in Lubelski's work (Plate 5)—are also dealing with failure in the realm of gender and gendered behavior.[11] Women who consume excessively have long been—and are still—framed as failed women: bad mothers, bad wives, bad girls. However, as Jack Halberstam reminds us: "From the perspective of feminism, failure has often been a better bet than success. Where feminine success is always measured by male standards, and gender failure often means being relieved of the pressure to measure up to patriarchal ideals, not succeeding at womanhood can offer unexpected pleasures. In many ways this has been the message of many renegade feminists in the past."[12] The concept of failure, considered in relation to, and as inextricably linked with, pleasure, will be woven throughout this chapter, as well as in the subsequent chapter on "bad women" artists. Halberstam observes that "this feminism, a feminism grounded in negation, refusal, passivity, absence, and silence, offers spaces and modes of unknowing, failing, and forgetting as part of an alternative feminist project, a shadow feminism which has nestled in more positivist accounts and unraveled their logics from within. This shadow feminism speaks in the language of self-destruction, masochism, an antisocial femininity."[13]

Figure 2.1 Orly Cogan, *Little Debbie I*, from Bachelor Girls/Sweet Confessions series, 2005. Vintage fabric, stitching, paint. 68.6 x 35.6 cm. Courtesy of the artist.

Chapter 2

Figure 2.2 Orly Cogan, *Little Debbie II*, from Bachelor Girls/Sweet Confessions series, 2005. Courtesy of the artist.

In *Professional Women Painters in Nineteenth-Century Scotland: Commitment, Friendship, Pleasure* (2000), Janice Helland remarks that

> although pleasure as a reading or viewing position has been theorized (often psychoanalytically), production is rarely looked at as work which gives pleasure. This is not to posit a romanticization of the role of the creative artist in society as a free worker or to suggest that the artist characterizes the non-alienated worker; rather I suggest that certain nineteenth-century women artists lived ordinary lives as cultural workers supporting themselves in a capitalist economy by following a career that gave them pleasure as well as income.[14]

Pleasure is central to the following discussion, and not only the pleasure that artists experience in the production of their art. If anything, I am more concerned with consumption and the pleasures inherent in feminist spectatorship. I propose that it is through representations and allusions to women's pleasure via the consumption of addictive substances (specifically cocaine and alcohol) that contemporary feminist artists such as Cogan and Lubelski are transforming or reinventing domestic textiles traditionally found in the kitchen. Cogan uses vintage textiles to create her erotic, humorous, and provocative works, while Lubelski, in works such as *Clumsy* (Plate 5), stitches textile stains into already-stained tablecloths. The stain, as several craft scholars have noted, is a loaded, gendered, and indeed classed piece of visual evidence.[15] In the context of pleasure, addictive substances, and craft, Lubelski has created a work that probes the tender recesses of domestic labor, women's needlework, and, as I discuss below, shame.[16]

The issue of pleasure is not new to the discourse of craft production and consumption. In his discussion of the Arts and Crafts movement in Britain in the late nineteenth century, Glenn Adamson underscores William Morris's and John Ruskin's interest in the affective aspects of handmade craft objects or handicrafts.[17] One affect of the artisanal experience, according to Morris and Ruskin, was the experience of pleasure in production, which differentiated handmade crafts from machine-made objects. Craft historian Sandra Alfoldy has also highlighted the fact that pleasure was part of Arts and Crafts discourse in the late Victorian period, as Morris's famous aphorism "Joy in Labour" indicates.[18]

Pleasure is sometimes accompanied by risks. Feminist artist and craft scholar Janis Jefferies has noted the risk inherent in working with craft materials for (women) artists based on the historical relationship between textiles and feminine stereotypes related to domesticity and obedience.[19] As Jefferies reminds us:

> For a woman artist to "return" as it were, to a prescribed traditional role in the minor arts (the decorative, craft and the domestic) generally less conducive to the fame and financial gain than a career in painting or sculpture, can be seen as a step backwards from a feminist point of view.[20]

Nonetheless, through the use of discursively loaded materials (fiber, ceramics, and rhinestones) and subject matter related to the consuming woman who seeks pleasure, works by Cogan and Lubelski, as well as by Mickalene Thomas and Shary Boyle, disrupt expectations about proper female behavior, and transgress boundaries of "appropriate" subject matter and materials for feminist art. Furthermore, the women within these works—whether present (represented as visible bodies) or absent (bodies signified by traces in the form of stains)—exceed gendered norms related to female identities and appropriate "feminine" behaviors.

Rozsika Parker observes in *The Subversive Stitch* that the "eighteenth century asserted that femininity was natural and that embroidery was the natural expression of femininity, but at least allowed that women achieved some satisfaction in embroidery. It was spoken of, even if mockingly, as a source of creative pleasure. In the nineteenth century, unless embroidery was performed as a moral duty, in the spirit of selfless industry, it was regarded as sinful laziness—redolent of aristocratic decadence."[21] Read as instances of *radical* decadence, the works of Cogan and Lubelski are, I suggest, activating what Race Kane has called "the critical agency of pleasure" by employing craft materials to depict women's consumption and (perceived) excess.[22]

Reinventing domestic textiles

I begin this section with a legal addictive substance—namely, alcohol—as "represented" in Asheville, N.C.-based Nava Lubelski's reinvented tablecloth artwork, *Clumsy* (Plate 5), and I will subsequently turn to an illicit addictive substance—namely, cocaine—that Orly Cogan has depicted more than once in her textile works.

According to the curator of the 2007 exhibition, *Pricked: Extreme Embroidery*:

> Memory, repair, and redemption are intertwined in the work of Nava Lubelski. Lubelski, whose anonymous narratives of time, place, and action become emblems of the inevitability of imperfection, works with the traces of accidents and mistakes using stained or damaged textiles. The artist recognizes the contradictions inherent in her work by transforming the unwanted and unintended markings of life into things of desirability and beauty. As the artist has said, "I experiment with the contradictions of spoiling and mending, using the healing notion of stitch to respond to stains and the imagery of contamination." A further contradiction in her work is Lubelski's intentional contrast between the patient and orderly process of needlework stitching with the spontaneous quality of spills and splashes.[23]

Lubelski's weaving together of women's alcohol consumption, stains, and textiles creates a symbolic site within which feminine stereotypes related to domesticity, shame, and the hierarchy of art and craft are all in motion and therefore volatile and unstable.

Joanna Frueh has remarked, "Drinking enhances the male artist. . . . The male artist drinker is supposedly wild, tough, devil-may-care, sexy, and dangerous: he is an icon of masculine ecstasy, the best kind of messiness. Never mind his self-absorbed chatter, egotism, and boring emotionalism, for they are not the stuff of myth, which shores up his mess. The female drunk is simply sloppy, self-indulgent, and sexually usable."[24] Later she comments that "messes may be signs of excess, the always unnecessary. . . . When women make a mess they do disturb the culturally imposed normalcy of female tidiness: don't smear your lipstick or run a stocking; don't let a bra-strap show or keep a sloppy household."[25] By producing artworks that employ already-stained domestic textiles, Lubelski unveils the belief that woman's mess = woman as mess. In *Clumsy,* she presents us with a large red stain that could be either wine or blood. Although there is no reference to alcohol in the title of *Clumsy*, the stain is usually interpreted as a wine stain.

The curator of *Pricked*, for example, writes that "*Clumsy* consists of a wine-stained tablecloth having a large central stain and multiple droplets of wine scattered over the surface. Each stain has been framed with delicate stitches of a brilliant red floss that alert the viewer to the overlooked potential for beauty in the accidental."[26] The term "delicate" speaks to Lubelski's skill as a craftsperson, and according to the curator, the main takeaway from the work is formal in nature: the "overlooked potential for beauty in the accidental." But this analysis leaves out the already-absent (female) drinker, the one who has spilled her red wine. The solitary stain suggests that she may have been drinking alone, though not necessarily. The work raises a number of unanswerable questions, all returning to the absent body of the female drinker and her drinking habits: Was she drinking alone? Why? How often does she drink alone? How many glasses of wine does she consume at a time? Why does she drink? How often does she drink? Why did she spill her wine? What time of day was she drinking? And why do any of these questions (and answers) matter, if they do matter? These are the questions, of course, that a medical professional might ask, or that an individual might ask herself if she is concerned about her drinking. They are the questions of a binge culture, within which a certain number of units of alcohol determine whether you are an excessive drinker or not.[27] The stain in (or on) Lubelski's textile work functions as a trace of the absent (female) drinker. And why do we assume that the drinker is female? Because the artist is female? Because the artwork comprises a type of textile traditionally associated with domesticity and therefore with women and women's work? Or is it because red wine is stereotypically a woman's drink, consumed at the end of a long, hard day at work?

Lubelski's artwork engages with histories of women's textile production, discourses of addiction, stereotypes related not only to "acceptable" or "respectable" femininity, but also to images of "unacceptable" or "subversive" femininity and feminism. Add popular culture to the mix, and we can read any number of bodies into the scene that Lubelski's reinvented tablecloth is at the center of—which brings to mind another question regarding the (female) drinker who has spilled her wine on the formerly pristine yellow tablecloth: If she was here but a few moments ago (long enough for the wine to drip down the side of the cloth), where has she gone, and why? In the next section I suggest that shame—and the discourses related to women's alcohol consumption that encourage, even demand, shame—may be part of the narrative inherent in Lubelski's work. But is the shame accepted or resisted?

Despite any hints of guilt or shame in *Clumsy*, Lubelski has produced a work that alludes to a subject—let us identify the subject as a woman—who consumes a legal, socially "acceptable" addictive substance. Cogan's reinvented textiles, on the other hand, represent women consuming an illicit addictive substance. As discussed in the previous chapter, Cogan has produced several works to date that represent young, white women who are consuming cupcakes and cocaine. In *Mirror, Mirror* (Plate 3), a clothed woman is portrayed snorting cocaine off a mirror, while in *Bittersweet Obsession* (Plate 2), women are depicted consuming both cupcakes and cocaine within the same pictorial space.

The curator of *Pricked* observes: "Orly Cogan has drawn, painted, and embroidered on an astonishing number and variety of found textiles. The artist finds fabrics—table linens, dresser scarves, pillowcases, bedsheets—that have previously been embroidered. Most often the embroidery work is clearly that of a hobby needleworker."[28] As I argued in Chapter 1, Cogan's juxtaposition of cupcakes and cocaine underscores the reality of many women's lives, in which they consume both licit, though symbolically loaded, foodstuffs (cakes and cupcakes) and illicit, addictive substances (including, but not limited to, cocaine). In portraying these acts of consumption on vintage domestic textiles in ironically retro pastel colors, Cogan has created humorous as well as subversive works that speak not of "drug abuse"[29]—despite at least one scholar's problematic use of this term in a discussion of Cogan's work[30]—but rather the complicated relationships that some women have with drugs.

I contend that Cogan's textile works representing women consuming both cupcakes and cocaine have been inadequately theorized by craft scholars and curators. This is perhaps not surprising given ongoing anxieties about women's drug use, and indeed feminist theorizations of women's drug use are still relatively rare.[31] Evidence that craft scholars are still somewhat uncomfortable with Cogan's drug-related subject matter is available in the texts that have been written about her work. For instance, Nadine Monem has commented:

> Cogan takes up the narrative of the fabric's past life in her found "canvases," taking the existing hand-embroidery on the old table runners, bureau scarves and tablecloths as conventions she can embellish to subvert. Flower motifs embedded in the cloth float around her stitched figures in a Gauguin Tahiti-like breeze as they embellish bodies but do nothing to cover up the intimate parts and gestures those bodies express. They seem to suggest a flux between the women's assertive and passive roles as they embrace and ignore each other with each passing fancy.[32]

This kind of analysis ignores the important critical work that Cogan is doing within a cultural context where the consumption of illicit drugs is still pathologized and penalized legally, in addition to her transgressive illumination of the fact that women *of all classes*— not just women of lower economic strata—consume illicit drugs for a range of reasons, including the desire for pleasure. More problematically, Monem remarks: "Cogan also directly explores issues around female identity and vice, . . . to depict themes of binge eating and drug abuse."[33] "Vice" is an outdated word that signifies both legally and morally, and "drug abuse" implies not only addiction, but also a more aggressively self-destructive behavior. The phrase not only erases the possibility of pleasure, but also shames the female subjects in Cogan's textiles and the female readers/viewers who may themselves consume cocaine. Furthermore, there is no reliable visual evidence of drug "abuse" *or* addiction in Cogan's works, as drug use is not synonymous with, nor is it necessarily indicative of, addiction. It is worth recalling Mary Russo's assertion that the "grotesque" woman in Western culture is still linked with "social and sexual deviances."[34] Further to this, Russo states that grotesque women—so often linked with "bodily excesses"—are framed as "repositories of shame and repressed desire."[35]

Stains and shame

Jenni Sorkin has argued that "cloth holds the sometimes unbearable gift of memory. And its memory is exacting: it does not forget even the benign scars of accident: red wine on a white tablecloth, water on a silk blouse, dark patches beneath the arms on a humid summer day."[36] In her theorization of stains, Sorkin makes several relevant observations, including the following: "*Stains mark the wearer:* To be stained is to be dirty, messy, poor, and/or careless. It infers a variety of judgments: One does not care for his or her clothing. One does not care about his or her presentation. One is unprofessional. One is obviously a slob. Many people feel embarrassment and/or scorn for the wearer of the stain. They hardly ever feel empathetic, preferring not to identify with the sloppy individual." And even more significantly, she remarks: "*Stains elicit shame:* . . . The self-stain renders the body uncontrollable: both capable and culpable of transmission, transgression and impurity, *exceeding the acceptable*, surpassing the boundaries of the skin."[37] She concludes: "Thus the embarrassment, discomfort, and humiliation of the self-stain can be excruciating, especially when the staining occurs publicly, or becomes public."[38] In a similar vein, Anne Hamlyn discusses Freud's writings on women, fetishism, textiles, and shame. As she remarks: "The problem of women's ambiguous relation both to fetishism and textiles is evident in one of Freud's most infamously misogynous passages from the paper 'Femininity' (1933)."[39] I want to argue that in unveiling the intersecting ideologies related to femininity, domesticity, alcohol, stains, and shame, Lubelski is engaging in a critique of these very ideologies, not simply celebrating pleasure in the form of consumption, but also pointing out the complications and risks inherent in pleasure via consumption, particularly for women. The viewer is implicated in this process, because although there is no body visible in the work, the absent subject is almost invariably assumed to be female. This is not simply or only because Lubelski is female; rather, I suggest, it is because this red stain signifies femininity of a disorderly kind. Dirt, or matter out of place, as Mary Douglas reminds us, is contained by society by identifying it as taboo and banishing it to the margins.[40] Lubelski places the stain at the center (metaphorically if not literally) of her domestic textile in order to critique viewing practices and belief systems that perceive the sloppy woman (and the female drinker/alcoholic) as threatening.

In Oscar Wilde's play *Salomé* (1891), which I discussed briefly in the Introduction, King Herod asserts at one point: "How red those petals are! They are like stains of blood on the cloth. That does not matter. It is not wise to find symbols in everything that one sees. It makes life too full of terrors. It were better to say that stains of blood are as lovely as rose petals."[41] Lubelski's stained tablecloth speaks both to these terrors (namely, the terror of the unruly, consuming woman) and to the coping strategies (including in art criticism) that attempt to turn stains into rose petals.

Look, but don't touch: Feminist spectatorship, pleasure, and feminist textiles

In a discussion of artists' engagement with craft materials in the 1960s and 1970s, Janis Jefferies observes:

> All depiction in painting and sculpture implies haptic response to some degree, but the concept of touch is much expanded in the works cited above, through specific choices of tactile or ephemeral materials. In this context, fabric, cloth and that which makes textile, is useful both as a material term and as a conceptual strategy operating in the transformative power of metaphor, interweaving between words and things, surfaces and skins, fibre and material, touch and tactility. In fact, the literature on aesthetics and art history focuses largely on sight to the exclusion of all other senses.[42]

Jefferies is not discussing Cogan or Lubelski, but her comments are pertinent to their work, because their reinvented domestic textiles, whether tablecloths or bed linens, speak to domestic activities that necessitate touch: cleaning, folding, unfolding, mending, and draping over tables and beds. Yet these works, as with all of the artworks discussed in *Radical Decadence*, are just that: *art*works. They are no longer "simply" domestic textiles. They were produced for visual consumption in museums and galleries, and, one might safely assume, for economic exchange that surpasses the price of actual or "everyday" tablecloths. As artworks, then, these textiles would be handled with kid gloves (literally and metaphorically) by museum professionals, and when on display in cultural institutions, touch—the haptic—would be prohibited.

If haptic pleasure is impossible with these works, except for the artists themselves—reminding us of the privileging of the "hand-made" in recent texts about craft[43]—and for art consumers who can afford to buy the works, what other avenues for pleasure are available to the (feminist) spectator? I want to suggest that these avenues exist, and they are multiple and intersecting. Certainly there is the vicarious pleasure of viewing women (or imagining women) consuming both baked goods and addictive substances that result in physiological pleasure. This particular "pathway" to pleasure[44] would necessarily depend on the viewer's experiences of consuming the specific foods represented (cakes and cupcakes in Cogan's works) and/or the addictive substances portrayed (cocaine in Cogan's textiles, red wine in Lubelski's *Clumsy*). There would be, then, a sense of identification, which may produce pleasure on the one hand, but also anxiety. Pleasure and anxiety are not, of course, mutually exclusive affects.[45]

A corollary avenue, a side path perhaps, is the vicarious pleasure of viewing women experiencing pleasure, even if that pleasure is complicated and ambivalent, as Cogan's titles, such as *Bittersweet Obsession*, suggest. However, I want to suggest once more that Cogan's works are not "merely" about shame, nor can they be easily dismissed as portraying women indulging in "guilty pleasures," a gendered phrase if ever there was one. Are these women shameless in their consumption and pleasure? Perhaps it is not as simple as identifying these female subjects as "ashamed" or "shameless." Rather, if we draw on Halberstam's queer/feminist theorization of failure, these women are "failing" *because* of their consumption, but as Halberstam proposes, there are unexpected rewards that go along with failure.[46] One of these rewards, of course, is pleasure: physiological pleasure, yes, but also the pleasure of resistance and subversion, of not bowing to gendered social expectations regarding behavior in general and consumption in particular. There are sometimes consequences, yes, but there are also unexpected paths that illuminate the world and its players in a way that would have been hidden (or veiled) if that path had not been taken.

Finally, a paradoxical pleasure suggested by these works is that of delayed gratification. We as viewers (not, significantly, *touchers*) can look at these works hung on the wall of galleries, or draped over tables in group exhibitions and installations, but we cannot—if we are well-behaved gallery-goers—touch them. The frisson of wanting to touch but not being allowed to touch: this proscription may result in the painful pleasure, or *la douleur exquise* (exquisite pain), of wanting something (or someone) that you cannot have, touch, or access. This of course unveils the sensual nature, the erotics, of (feminist) spectatorship, and in the context of the museum and gallery, the fundamental proscription of touch speaks directly to the experience of unrequited love, the impossibility of getting what one wants, and the painful pleasure that goes along with that experience. Kane Race has remarked:

> In order to understand the field of gay men's responses to HIV/AIDS, I draw on certain insights from corporeal feminism, which, among its other contributions, has developed a different perspective on the possibilities of agency and responsibility than that which is prescribed within medico-moral regimes. In particular, corporeal feminism has developed a notion of ethical agency that is grounded in specific habits of embodiment and practices of inhabitation. This concept of ethics contrasts with conventional understandings that cast ethics as a universal set of principles that are grasped and applied by the rational mind in a disciplinary feat of mind over matter. From the corporeal perspective, ethics are grounded in specific practices of embodiment that are historically conditioned.[47]

For contemporary feminist artists, desire, pleasure, and indeed failure appear to be inextricably wound up together in a complicated matrix that is not completely shame-free, nor guilty (thereby rejecting the absurd phrase "guilty pleasures"), but speaks to a restlessness, or a relentless seeking, after *more*: more pleasure, more resistance, more subversion, more consumption, more transformation.

The "lure of the surface": Shary Boyle and Mickalene Thomas

As Moira Vincentelli has observed, "Surface decoration is frequently seen as 'mere' decoration and characterised as superficial, meaningless and lacking in intellectual rigour."[48] The artists discussed in this section are working against this historical vision of surface, which has been closely aligned with women and women's bodies. The "lure of the surface" is Anne Anlin Cheng's phrase, which she uses in her study of Josephine Baker and modernism's desire for both the racialized black (female) body and for transparency.[49] According to Cheng, "Baker's incandescent, sculptural figure also urges us to turn to another 'cult of light': the discourse of 'shine' and sculptural surfaces in the 1920s and 1930s."[50] She adds that "through shine itself, artists believed they could release sculpture from its material condition and open it up to new meanings."[51]

Art historian Hal Foster theorizes "sheen" in his essay "The Art of Fetishism: Notes on Dutch Still Life." In this well-known article, Foster discusses "pronk" paintings, "lavish displays of fine objects and extravagant food (in Dutch *pronken* means 'to show off'). If only a superficial sheen or shine, this visual intensity cannot be explained away as an effect of a disguised symbolism or a residue of a religious gaze; a fetishistic projection on the part of artist and viewer alike is involved."[52] Dutch pronk paintings, or *Vanitas* paintings (see Figure 4.2), were representations of luxury items, foodstuffs, and general abundance, but coded with hints about transience and mortality—the fruit is just this side of decay, an hourglass reminds us that we only have so many days left to live, a fragile bubble floats in the air. These examples of memento mori, in representing material excess, signaled to the viewer that all was transience and, in doing so, reminded the viewer of his or her immortal soul. As Foster writes, "Certainly in pronk pieces the concern with social position, with excess and ostentation, or, even less generous, the emphasis on moral probity, on 'remonstrance against excess and ostentation,' overwhelms the sense of offering or gift vestigial in still life."[53] He goes on to state that "the viewer may revel in this consumption but see it controlled, not only through the caution of destructive excess or implicit *Vanitas* but also by skilled craft."[54] For Foster, our gaze reflected in the "luminous shine" of pronk paintings is "Medusal" in that it "looks back from things, and threatens us."[55]

Shary Boyle's porcelain sculpture *To Colonize the Moon* (Plate 6) portrays the decapitated head of a woman with writhing snakes for hair. This Medusal woman gazes at a naked male youth who holds a sword and is seated next to a round mirror. This work combines various "decadent" themes and figures, including the mirror, the male youth, and Medusa. The combination of a mirror and a beautiful young man reminds us of Narcissus, although Boyle was thinking of another mythic youth when she produced the work. The porcelain sculpture is a response to Florentine artist Battista Foggini's bronze sculpture, *Perseus Slaying Medusa* (mid-seventeenth–early eighteenth century), which is in the Art Gallery of Ontario's collection. The woman with viper tresses in Boyle's work is no longer much of a threat to the young man, as she is already decapitated. The entire sculpture, including the woman's face and the youth's body, glistens with a "luminous shine." I would suggest that Boyle is playing here with myths (and ideologies) that frame women as threatening, employing traditional porcelain techniques and shiny surfaces to depict a mythological scene that shows the aftermath of male violence toward a monstrous woman.

In his discussion of fetishism and decadence, Charles Bernheimer critically examines Wilde's *Salomé*, in which the eponymous character demands the head of St John the Baptist, in relation to Freud's theories of castration, which Bernheimer argues is "the seminal fantasy of the decadent imagination."[56] I will jump right to the last two lines of Bernheimer's essay and quote his belief that "castration is theory's decadent fetish. It is high time to discard it on the compost heap of history."[57] Bernheimer, of course, is concerned with male decadent imaginations, particularly, though not exclusively, Wilde's. As I discussed in the Introduction, feminist scholars and women artists and designers have had different motivations and preoccupations when it comes to decadence. None of the artists discussed in this book, I would argue, are interested in castration. The fetish, too, I think, has lost some of its luster as a way of theorizing or interpreting visual material, especially that by women. Therefore, I will gloss over Bernheimer's discussion of the fetish, to focus on his discussion of surfaces, which, in the context of works by Boyle and Thomas, is much more suggestive. Like Foster, Bernheimer's discussion returns again and again to glittering surfaces. As he notes of J. K. Huysmans's *A rebours*, in which the novelist described Gustave Moreau's depictions of Salome: "Foreshadowing Freud, he offers himself the consolation of constructing the petrified Salome as a gleaming, brilliant fetish. . . . She is like a highly ornamental sculpture."[58] Later, he refers to "dazzling surface effects."[59]

My argument about the optical effects—including sheen—in works by Mickalene Thomas and Shary Boyle is rather different from Foster's and Bernheimer's, but it is indebted to Cheng's. Although it could be said that our gaze bounces back from the shiny surfaces of sculptures by Boyle (Figure 2.3) and Thomas (Figure 2.4), I want to suggest that both artists' works engage with histories of female and nonwhite bodies, as

Figure 2.3 Shary Boyle, *Untitled*, 2005. Lace-draped porcelain and china paint. 27 × 20 × 20.5 cm. National Gallery of Canada, Ottawa. Courtesy of the artist.

Figure 2.4 Mickalene Thomas, *Brawlin' Spitfire Wrestlers 2*, 2008. Resin, paint, and Swarovski crystals. 10 × 14 × 9.75 in. © Mickalene Thomas. Courtesy of Mickalene Thomas and Artists Rights Society (ARS), New York.

well as current realities, and in doing so, they make visible the ideologies that are often invisible: the misogyny that renders women monstrous for transgressing social norms and proscriptions, as well as the racism underlying the hypersexualization of the black female body in representation. By making these ideologies visible in material, three-dimensional objects, Boyle and Thomas create works that are pleasurable to look at for feminist spectators who know not only the histories of (both black and white) women and women's bodies, but also the historical connotations of ceramics and other craft materials.[60]

Thomas and Boyle play with shine (or sheen) in their sculptural works, as well as in Thomas's mixed media works that incorporate rhinestones.[61] In Boyle's ceramic sculptures, women are rendered monstrous, often through excess: their foreheads are full of eyes, they have too many arms, or their heads have been cut off, again recalling both the Medusa myth and the story of Salome and John the Baptist. In *Untitled* (2004, National Gallery of Canada), a woman with multiple eyes and multiple arms holds myriad threads in her fingers, spinning like Arachne who was turned into a spider by Athena for boasting that she could weave better than the goddess. As Rebecca Solnit has written, "Ancient Greek stories included an unfortunate spinning woman who was famously turned into a spider as well as the more powerful Greek fates, who spun, wove, and cut each person's lifeline, who ensured that those lives would be linear narratives that end.

Spiderwebs are images of the non-linear, of the many directions in which something can go, the many sources for it; of the grandmothers as well as the strings of begats."[62]

All of Boyle's sculptural female figures wear beautiful, ornate costumes that recall, deliberately and ironically, the eighteenth-century porcelain figurines that Boyle parodies and reinvents:

> Boyle's porcelains have a very direct historical precedent. Her approach to the medium is closely aligned with the Meissen technique that developed in Germany in the early 1700s. The figures manufactured in the Meissen factory bore the traits of the decorative and ornate Rococo period, which superseded the Baroque style favoured in the previous century. Though Rococo elements are evident in Boyle's decorative lacework, beaded accoutrements and intricate surface glazing, her content veers from the lighthearted imagery of their eighteenth-century precedents.[63]

In another untitled work (Figure 2.3), the female subject is being consumed by her own mutating lace dress: "The dress is laden with excessive layers of the delicate fabric, which is also grafted onto the figure's face and hand."[64] This work, in demonstrating Boyle's skill in the lace-draping technique, also points up ideals of femininity and the absurdity of women's dress throughout history. As Boyle herself has commented, the decoration of porcelain figures is "perversely ornate and beautiful but in the way of excessive femininity that is just bizarre."[65]

Thomas's *Brawlin' Spitfire Wrestlers 2* (Figure 2.4) portrays glistening black female subjects in strenuous, active poses, and is made of resin, paint, and Swarovski crystal. The use of luxurious materials (crystal), in addition to the painted sheen of the black bodies, speaks to an awareness of the pleasures inherent in surfaces and in looking at these surfaces. In other words, both Boyle and Thomas are acutely aware of the "lure of the surface," but with distinct histories attached to their raced bodies. Whiteness, of course, is a race.[66] For instance, in Thomas's sculpture, the animal-print leotards speak to the history of black women being represented as hypersexual, animalistic, and savage.[67] In *Brawlin' Spitfire Wrestlers 2*, this alleged "savagery" is sublimated through an image of strong black women wrestling; their leotards parody the ways that black women were historically represented as both primitive and subhuman.

In Thomas's paintings, she employs specific materials not only to seduce the eye, but also to do critical, subversive work. Her use of rhinestones to portray the heavily madeup subject in *Are You That Someone?* (Plate 7) draws the viewer's attention to the woman's eyelids, lips, hair, jewelry, and clothing, the "surfaces" that serve as the materials of self-fashioning.[68] According to Ellen Rudolph, "Thomas addresses exoticized stereotypes of black femininity while also exploring how her women fit into art history, which has traditionally relegated black women to subservient, peripheral roles. She looks at black female sexuality from her perspective as an African-American woman whose notions of beauty and femininity were formed while she was growing up in New Jersey in the 1970s and 1980s."[69]

In Thomas's *I Learned the Hard Way* (Plate 8), which is part of the series *Put a Little Sugar in My Bowl*, a woman, possibly in her fifties, perches upon a bed or sofa.[70] She wears a golden headdress and an elegant purple dress with a golden collar; historically, these are the colors of royalty. The woman is composed and dignified, and the title hints at a hard life, or at least a significant event that allows her to acknowledge a mistake, or failure, and to state that she has "learned the hard way." The work is also full of clashing textiles and patterns—at least eight different patterns are visible and they are noticeably and deliberately jarring.[71] Like in Boyle's ceramic figures, textiles are part of the painting's surface, as well as part of its discursive work. In Thomas's paintings they are flat, and in Boyle's sculptures they are three-dimensional, but the textiles emphasize one aspect of the works' "excessiveness," linking them to the decorative arts and women's craft that, as we have seen throughout *Radical Decadence*, have both been perceived and framed as excessive. Now, in the twenty-first century, and not for the first time, feminist artists are deliberately embracing the ostensible excessiveness of textiles, craft, and the decorative to critique not only aesthetic and art-historical categories, but also ideologies of gender and race.

What exactly makes Thomas's and Boyle's works "excessive"? For Thomas, her use of rhinestones (a material associated with kitschy or fake jewelry) and crystals (a material associated with luxury) creates a juxtaposition of high and low. Furthermore, these materials are added to the surface of her paintings and sculptures; they *are* surface, decorative, and are "in excess" of paint. Thomas is well-versed in art history, and has cited Manet and Matisse, as well as Carrie Mae Weems, as influences.[72] In a 2011 interview with artist Sean Landers, Thomas noted that in criticism written about her art, it is rare that her wood panel works are described as paintings. This fact is significant in the context of women artists using materials that have historically been associated with craft. It also says something troubling about the reception of women artists generally, and women artists of color in particular. Indeed, African American artist Faith Ringgold had the same experience in the early 1970s, when she was producing paintings inspired by Tibetan *thangka*, "a form of religious painting on silk set within a wide, hanging brocade frame."[73] According to Ringgold, "There were people who were confused by these tankas; they called them weavings, banners, textiles, fibers. They didn't seem to realize they were looking at paintings on canvas."[74] When Landers asked Thomas why she thinks critics do not perceive her works as paintings, she responded: "It could be that the materials I use are too seductive and all-consuming, but that's a part of the concept. People get so caught up with the rhinestones. The rhinestones are really just one part of the work among many. They are a way of masking things and they refer to the idea of artifice."[75] Significantly, both masking and artifice were part of the discourse of decadence in the late nineteenth century.[76]

The disdain for "craft" materials is evident in the Landers/Thomas interview. Couched as support for her work, Landers comments that "I love your work in this stage [i.e., pre-rhinestones]. Whenever you feel ready to not bedazzle them, go straight ahead, because the painting is good enough."[77] This statement is so patently belittling that it takes one's breath away. It also misses the point. Considering the history of the black female body in both representation and lived culture, which I discuss in the next section of this chapter, Thomas's use of rhinestones to "mask" her black female subjects is in fact a brilliant and critical move. While the rhinestones seem, on the surface, to draw attention to the subjects' faces, hair, and clothes, they also interrupt, or interfere with, the viewer's gaze, effectively disrupting the viewer's desired access to the black women's faces and bodies. The lure of the surface, here, is actually a mask or even a shield. Thomas knew exactly what she was talking about when she stated that the rhinestones in her paintings are "a way of masking things." The rhinestones are not superfluous to her work; they are crucial.

The female subject in *Are You that Someone?* is, like other female subjects in Thomas's paintings, heavily made up. Excess, as we know, is not only subjective but also culturally contingent. I am not arguing that the women in Thomas's paintings *are* excessive, but that Thomas is playing with the idea of excess in the materials she uses and the way she represents her black female subjects as self-fashioning through makeup, clothing, and interiors. Cosmetics were identified as decadent by male writers in the late nineteenth century, albeit problematically, because they often described women in misogynistic terms. According to Charles Baudelaire, for instance, makeup was to be praised as it permitted women to construct themselves as fetishes, as "dazzling, shiny surface[s]" that cover over and obscure "the corrupt sexual nature beneath."[78] Statements like this one remind us that decadence, as envisioned by male writers and artists in the late nineteenth century, was not kind to women, and it had to be radically transformed by women artists and designers in the early twentieth century,[79] and by feminist scholars more recently, in order to be considered as a productive, liberating aesthetic and lived experience. According to Bernheimer, "Etymologically, the fetish is a decadent object. . . . The French word *maquillage*, 'makeup', is semantically connected to 'fetish' through the Germanic root *maken*, 'to make'. As a verb, *maquiller*, like the words deriving from *facticius*, suggests not just painting one's face but also to fake, disguise, mask."[80] What this passage and his entire essay leave out, of course, is women's agency as artists "making up" or "making art" that engages with dress, ornament, and cosmetics as a form of self-reflexive radical decadence.

For Boyle, whose ceramic women so often have too many of something—eyes, arms, or heads, the better to self-pleasure with, as in *Ouroboros* (Plate 9)—there is a desire to create monstrous women who make visible the ideologies that render women grotesque and monstrous, as discussed in Chapter 1, for consuming, desiring, and exceeding. Furthermore, ceramics have historically been linked with both women and (perceived) excess, making them a highly symbolic material for a feminist artist. Stacey Sloboda has discussed how ceramic objects were gendered as feminine and associated with excessive consumption by female consumers in the eighteenth century.[81] The history of ceramics as perceived objects of craft rather than art once again speaks to the art/craft hierarchy. Like Cogan and Lubelski, then, Boyle and Thomas are producing feminist artworks that engage with materials traditionally associated not only with craft, but also with gendered behaviors and activities that were linked, in turn, with gendered and raced excess.

In the eighteenth century, ceramics were regarded as "Oriental" because of the originary source of many of the ceramic objects purchased by British women of the court. Cheng remarks that "the primitive black woman is all about exposed nakedness, while the 'Oriental' woman is all about sartorial excess, the excessive covering and ornamentation that supposedly symptomizes the East's overly developed, effeminized, corrupt, and declining civilization."[82] She goes on to observe: "There is, in fact, a longstanding intimacy between the discourse of nineteenth-century European Decadence and Orientalism, often signaled by an excessive preoccupation with fabrics."[83] These insights bring into focus the interwoven threads of decadence, ceramics, women, consumption, and textiles that I have been concerned with in this chapter.[84] Sloboda comments that "the exuberant, ornamentally excessive style of chinoiserie materialized the concept of disorder, rhetorically binding it to femininity."[85] Just as feminist artists working with textiles are drawing on, as well as subverting, histories and connotations of historical textile objects made by women, feminist artists working with ceramics—particularly those that represent gendered and raced subjects—are both engaging with and pushing against the historical significations of porcelain. Significantly, in the eighteenth century, the consumption and collection of chinoiserie ceramics provided a potential site of female agency, as Sloboda points out. Sloboda observes, citing the work of David Porter, that Chinese objects may also have been appealing to eighteenth-century women because they sometimes visualized a utopian female space: "When viewed against the backdrop of the dominant European tradition, these Chinese designs conjure up a protected utopian space of female dignity, autonomy, intimate community, and pleasure that is relatively inaccessible within the imaginative confines of Western visual iconography."[86]

The black female body in context

In order to understand the critical, radical work that Thomas in particular is doing with her paintings and sculptures, it is important to further illuminate the history of the black female subject in visual and material culture. Art historian Charmaine Nelson has written of how nineteenth-century sculpture, marble sculpture specifically, was part of racializing discourses that were inextricably linked with discourses related to artistic taste, slavery, and gender. According to Nelson, the very whiteness of neoclassical marble sculpture highlights the privileging of whiteness as a race. As Nelson observes, "The whiteness of the marble medium was not of arbitrary significance but functioned to mediate the representation of the racialized body in ways that preserved a moral imperative essential to the ideals of nineteenth-century neoclassicism."[87] She goes on to state that "morality, then, was the measure of 'good' art, which was produced through the disavowal of the biological body, which was also the sexual and racial body. Marble was not incidental but critical to the process of representation, since it facilitated the fetishization of the body, representing it in a moral guise that could be visually understood as art."[88] Ultimately, she concludes that "what the white marble of nineteenth-century neoclassical sculpture really suppressed was the possibility of the representation of the black body, which registered racial-color difference at the level of the skin."[89]

As Cheng reminds us, "Especially when it comes to representations of women and racial minorities, the visual is almost always negatively inflected and usually seen as a tool of commoditization and objectification."[90] Implicit in this statement, of course, is the commoditization and objectification of the black slave body. Nelson discusses the representation of the slave body in neoclassical sculpture in *The Color of Stone: Sculpting* the *Black Female Subject in Nineteenth-Century America* (2007), and Marcus Wood has suggested that engravings that represent black female slaves being punished in eighteenth-century abolitionist texts are often pornographic in objectifying the suffering black female subject.[91] Many scholars have noted the revulsion and attraction that white spectators felt looking at black bodies at various points in history, whether female slaves or the Hottentot Venus.[92] During the period that slavery was still commonplace in both Europe and the United States, this revulsion/attraction manifested in black individuals being perceived as subhuman, which resulted in rampant sexual abuse toward black female slaves by white male slave owners. As Nelson suggests, this endemic sexual violence was inextricably tied to the constant representation of black women, in "high" and "low" art, "as sexually excessive, immoral and licentious."[93] Later, when slavery had been abolished, the revulsion went underground—though certainly did not disappear as ongoing racism and hate crimes, from lynchings to police shootings, attest—and the attraction became more acceptable. For instance, in the 1920s in Paris, as Petrine Archer-Straw has discussed, "Negrophilia," the desire not only for black bodies but also for black culture, was a major part of the avant-garde scene.[94] Negrophilia, of course, influenced the work of canonical male modernists such as Picasso, whose interest in African masks is evident in *Les Demoiselles d'Avignon* (1907). It was in 1920s Paris that Josephine Baker, a woman from St. Louis in the United States, became famous for her "exotic" and "savage" dances, what Cheng call's Baker's "relentless self-fetishization."[95] Cheng remarks that the "politics of embodiment and subjectivity for a woman of color has always been a tricky business."[96] She adds that "Baker constantly gives us surface rather than body."[97] With the materials that she has chosen, one might argue that Thomas is playing a similar, serious trick.

Conclusion: Boyle's monstrous, self-pleasuring woman

In her sculpture *Ouroboros* (Plate 9), a term that refers to the alchemical symbol of a snake or lizard eating its own tail (this symbol comes up again in the next chapter), Boyle depicts a freckled, red-haired woman on her back, her legs in the air, with an arch of her own heads connected so that she is portrayed performing oral sex on herself. Like Boyle's other female subjects, this woman wears a beautiful dress that recalls traditional ceramic figurines that were once elite objects and are now largely relegated to grandmothers' mantelpieces. The repetition of the head—suggesting a reflection upon a reflection in a series of mirrors—and the act of self-love alludes to the story of Narcissus and the concept of narcissism. Bernheimer asserts that the "fetish returns the gaze from the depths of symbolic meaning to the glittering details of the aesthetic surface. . . . The shiny surface is like a mirror, perhaps the most widespread of decadent fetishes."[98] For women, the mirror has long been a symbol of vanity, but in Cogan's *Mirror, Mirror*, this object, "the most widespread of decadent fetishes," is no longer a symbol of woman's vanity. It is no longer a symbol at all. It is merely a surface from which to snort cocaine. In Boyle's *Ouroboros*, there is no visible mirror, but the repeated head suggests reflection. According to Bernheimer, "In decadence . . . creative energy finds itself framed in a mirror of reflection and repetition. The mirror is full of already painted masks; the artist's belatedness stares him [sic] in the face like the knot of serpents swarming around Medusa's head."[99] The act of masturbation, of course, implies that no other human is needed for sexual pleasure. Whether or not that is perceived as threatening, the decadent woman, the monstrous woman, the grotesque woman, the excessive woman, is one who seeks pleasure (among other things) *despite* societal proscriptions. In a discussion of artist Sylvie Fleury's luxury-related installations, Anne Hamlyn remarks that her work exhibits "an excessive self-pleasuring that effectively turns the tables on any viewer too quick to pass judgment."[100] This "excessive" self-pleasuring may come in the form of shopping, drinking, snorting cocaine, eating, or masturbation, which Boyle's *Ouroboros* humorously nods to with her many-headed woman who is able to give herself head.

Some (feminist) viewers will experience a great deal of pleasure looking at these works, in part because of the artists' skill, the materials used, the optical effects, and the represented or implied acts of consumption. Other viewers will feel uncomfortable, unimpressed, anxious, or disgusted. This is to be expected with works engaged in the project of radical decadence. The artworks discussed in this chapter demonstrate that, although women's pleasure may have consequences—physical (hangovers), financial (debt), social (getting a "bad" reputation), and affective (guilt, shame)—women continue to consume for pleasure, as we always have, and feminist artists not afraid of excess are portraying consumption and its concomitant pleasures in textiles, porcelain, paint, and rhinestones.

Notes

1 See Rosemary Betterton, "Body Horror?: Food (and Sex and Death) in Women's Art," in *An Intimate Distance: Women, Artists and the Body*, 130–60.

2 Elissa Auther, *String, Felt, Thread: The Hierarchy of Art and Craft in American Art* (Minneapolis and London: University of Minnesota Press, 2010), xv.

3 Joanna Frueh, "Making a Mess: Women's Bane, Women's Pleasure," in Katy Deepwell (ed.), *Women Artists and Modernism* (Manchester and New York: Manchester University Press, 1998), 142.

4 Ibid., 154.

5 Ibid., 152.

6 Many women artists have, since the early twentieth century, represented themselves and other women smoking cigarettes in paintings and photographs, from Gluck in the 1920s to Sarah Lucas in the 1990s. Whereas the cigarette has long been deemed acceptable as subject matter—or prop—in paintings, women's consumption of cocaine has been largely the purview of other media and materials (such as film and textile art). Male artists have frequently represented women consuming alcohol in graphic art (e.g., William Hogarth's *Gin Lane*, 1751) and paintings (Otto Dix's *Portrait of Journalist Sylvia von Harden*, 1926), but female artists representing women drinking alcohol are much less common. On representations of women smoking, see Sharon Anne Cook, *Canadian Women, Smoking, and Visual Culture, 1880-2000* (Montreal and Kingston: McGill-Queen's University Press, 2012).

7 Frueh, "Making a Mess," 152.

8 Judith Mastai, "The Anorexic Body: Contemporary Installation Art by Women Artists in Canada," in Griselda Pollock (ed.), *Generations and Geographies in the Visual Arts: Feminist Readings* (London and New York: Routledge, 1996), 136.

9 Ibid., 142.

10 Ibid., 144.

11 See Mary Russo, *The Female Grotesque: Risk, Excess and Modernity* (New York and London: Routledge, 1994).

12 Judith Halberstam, *The Queer Art of Failure* (Durham, NC, and London: Duke University Press, 2011), 4.

13 Ibid., 124. Feminist craft scholar Janis Jefferies has suggested that "dangerous, vulnerable, angry, chaotic and multifariously defined desires" have been, and continue to be, "conjured by textile metaphors, processes and materials." Jefferies, "Textiles," 198.

14 Janice Helland, *Professional Women Painters in Nineteenth-Century Scotland: Commitment, Friendship, Pleasure* (Aldershot, UK, and Brookfield, VT: Ashgate, 2000), 8.

15 See, for instance, Sorkin, "Stain: On Cloth, Stigma, and Shame," 59–63. Originally published as Sorkin, "Stain: On Cloth, Stigma, and Shame," *Third Text* 14, no. 53 (2000): 77–80.

16 For more on women, addictive substances, and shame, see Julia Skelly, *Wasted Looks: Addiction and British Visual Culture, 1751-1919* (Burlington, VT: Ashgate, 2014), Chapter 1.

17 Glenn Adamson, *The Invention of Craft* (London and New York: Bloomsbury, 2013), xx. See also Anthea Callen, *Women in the Arts and Crafts Movement, 1870-1914* (London: Astragal Books, 1980).

18 Sandra Alfoldy, *The Allied Arts: Architecture and Craft in Postwar Canada* (Montreal and Kingston: McGill-Queen's University Press, 2012), 6.

19 Rozsika Parker and Griselda Pollock, *Old Mistresses: Women, Art and Ideology* (London: Routledge and Kegan Paul, 1981), 65.

20 Jefferies, "Contemporary Textiles," 44.

21 Rozsika Parker, *The Subversive Stitch: Embroidery and the Making of the Feminine* (1984; London and New York: I.B. Tauris, 2010), 153–54.

22 Kane Race, *Pleasure Consuming Medicine: The Queer Politics of Drugs* (Durham, NC, and London: Duke University Press, 2009), ix.

23 *Pricked: Extreme Embroidery* (New York: Museum of Arts and Design, 2007), 58.

24 Frueh, "Making a Mess," 151.

25 Ibid., 153.

26 *Pricked*, 58.

27 Martin Plant and Moira Plant, *Binge Britain: Alcohol and the National Response* (Oxford: Oxford University Press, 2006).

28 *Pricked*, 76.

29 "These investments converge most forcefully in the legal construction of 'drug abuse', which, though high-profile practices of patrol and reportage, is liable to manifest as an offensive example of self-administration." Kane, *Pleasure Consuming Medicine*, 60.

30 Monem, *Contemporary Textiles: The Fabric of Fine Art*, 75.

31 For exceptions, see Susan C. Boyd, *From Witches to Crack Moms: Women, Drug Law, and Policy* (Durham, NC: Carolina Academic Press, 2004), and Skelly, *Wasted Looks*. Race's methodology in *Pleasure Consuming Medicine* draws productively on queer theory, and it provides a useful critical model for feminist theorists concerned with women's drug use and addiction, whether in visual culture or in lived experience.

32 Monem, *Contemporary Textiles*, 74.

33 Ibid., 75.

34 Russo, *The Female Grotesque*, 14.

35 Ibid., 24.

36 Sorkin, "Stain: On Cloth, Stigma, and Shame," 59.

37 Ibid., 60. Emphasis added.

38 Ibid.

39 Anne Hamlyn, "Freud, Fabric, Fetish," in Hemmings (ed.), *The Textile Reader*, 20. Originally published as Hamlyn, "Freud, Fabric, Fetish," *Textile: The Journal of Cloth and Culture* 1, no. 1 (2003): 9–27.

40 Mary Douglas, *Purity and Danger: An Analysis of Concepts of Pollution and Taboo* (1966; London and New York: Routledge, 2001).

41 Quoted in Bernheimer, "Fetishism and Decadence: Salome's Severed Heads," 80.

42 Jefferies, "Contemporary Textiles," 38.

43 See, for example, Shu Hung and Joseph Magliaro (eds), *By Hand: The Use of Craft in Contemporary Art* (New York: Princeton Architectural Press, 2007). "The participants profiled in this book all share a dedication to materials and processes. They admit to spending months on a single piece with no end in sight and, in fact, luxuriate in their long production time" (7).

44 According to Kane Race, "Normative models of reward pathways riddle the popular and scientific literature on addiction, while as early as the 1940s, the concept of anhedonia (literally, the inability to feel pleasure) was being cited in American psychiatry in order to prescribe certain patients speed." Race, *Pleasure Consuming Medicine*, xi–xii.

45 See Valerie Traub, *Desire and Anxiety: Circulations of Sexuality in Shakespearean Drama* (New York and London: Routledge, 1992).

46 Halberstam, *The Queer Art of Failure*.

47 Race, *Pleasure Consuming Medicine*, 108.

48 Moira Vincentelli, *Women and Ceramics: Gendered Vessels* (Manchester and New York: Manchester University Press, 2000), 77.

49 Anne Anlin Cheng, *Second Skin: Josephine Baker and the Modern Surface* (Oxford and New York: Oxford University Press, 2011), 162.

50 Ibid., 115.

51 Ibid.

52 Hal Foster, "The Art of Fetishism: Notes on Dutch Still Life," in Apter and Pketz (eds), *Fetishism as Cultural Discourse*, 253.

53 Ibid., 258.

54 Ibid., 260.

55 Ibid., 264–65.

56 Bernheimer, "Fetishism and Decadence," 62.

57 Ibid., 83.

58 Ibid., 68.

59 Ibid., 69.

60 Louise Déry comments: "Shary Boyle deploys a seductive skill in bringing the beauty of bodies and faces to light. She appeals to the senses and to the emotions in order to lift the opaque covering from taboos and wounds. No effort is spared: the lustre of glossy paint, the brilliance of the porcelain, the alluring texture of the tiny polymer miniatures, the fluidity of the lace and ribbons, the gleam of the polychrome flesh and delicate gilding." Louise Déry (ed.), "The Redemption of the Senses," in *Shary Boyle: Flesh and Blood* (Montreal: Galerie l'UQAM, 2010), 106.

61 I have found several texts particularly useful for shaping my methodological approach as a white feminist art historian writing about black women artists. These texts include Patricia Hill Collins's *Black Feminist Thought: Knowledge, Consciousness, and the Politics of Empowerment* (New York: Routledge, 1990), bell hooks's *Black Looks: Race and Representation* (Toronto: Between the Lines, 1992), and Belinda Edmondson's essay "Black Aesthetics, Feminist Aesthetics, and the Problems of Oppositional Discourse," in Hilary Robinson (ed.), *Feminist/Art/Theory: An Anthology 1968-2000* (Massachusetts: Blackwell Publishing, 2001), 325–41.

62 Rebecca Solnit, "Grandmother Spider," in *Men Explain Things to Me* (Chicago: Haymarket Books, 2014), 81.

63 Michelle Jacques, "Art and History," in Déry (ed.), *Shary Boyle: Flesh and Blood*, 134–35.

64 Josée Drouin-Brisebois, "Ornamental Impulse," in Shary Boyle and Josée Drouin-Brisebois (eds), *Otherworld Uprising* (Montreal: Conundrum Press, 2008), 28.

65 Quoted in ibid., 36.

66 See Richard Dyer, *White: Essays on Race and Culture* (London and New York: Routledge, 1997).

67 Sander Gilman, "The Hottentot and the Prostitute: Toward an Iconography of Female Sexuality," in Kymberly N. Pinder (ed.), *Race-ing Art History: Critical Readings in Race and Art History* (New York and London: Routledge, 2002), 121–26.

68 See Kobena Mercer, "Black Hair/Style Politics," in Russell Ferguson, Martha Gever, Trinh T. Min-ha, and Cornel West (eds), *Out There: Marginalization and Contemporary Cultures* (New York: The New Museum of Contemporary Art, 1990), 247–64.

69 Ellen Rudolph (ed.), "The Cultural Currency of Pattern and Dress," in *Pattern ID* (Akron, OH: Akron Art Museum, 2010), 14.

70 Thomas bases her paintings on photographs that she takes of her carefully selected models.

71 In a discussion that touches on Thomas's work, Cecilia Gunzburger Anderson remarks that "textiles used to furnish interior spaces extend the same issues of social identity communicated by clothing beyond the body and into the environment." Cecilia Gunzburger Anderson, "We Are What We Wear: Cross-Cultural Uses of Textiles," *Pattern ID* (Akron, OH: Akron Art Museum, 2010), 74. She observes that the women represented in Thomas's *Girlfriends and Lovers* occupy a space filled with "boldly patterned 1960s and 1970s interior fabrics. The striped fabric in the center background bears Egyptian-esque symbols, a nod to the Africanist sensibilities in the African-American community of the 1970s, while the other large-scale stylized patterns and the Persian-inspired tablecloth were associated with an avant-garde, youthful, or counterculture clientele, reflecting then-current fashion and a reaction against the floral chintzes of affluent mainstream interiors" (74).

72 Rudolph, "The Cultural Currency of Pattern and Dress," 15.

73 Auther, *String, Felt, Thread*, 103.

74 Quoted in ibid., 106.

75 Sean Landers, "Mickalene Thomas," *Bomb*, no. 116 (Summer 2011), http://bombmagazine. org/article/5105/mickalene-thomas (last accessed July 2, 2015).

76 Max Beerbohm's "A Defence of Cosmetics" (1894) satirized the decadent cult of artifice. Max Beerbohm, "A Defence of Cosmetics," in Karl Beckson (ed.), *Aesthetes and Decadents of the 1890's* (Chicago: Academy Chicago Publishers, 1993), 48–63.

77   Landers, "Mickalene Thomas."

78   Bernheimer, "Fetishism and Decadence," 63.

79   Jasmine Rault, *Eileen Gray and the Design of Sapphic Modernity: Staying In* (Farnham, UK, and Burlington, VT: Ashgate, 2011).

80   Bernheimer, "Fetishism and Decadence," 63.

81   Stacey Sloboda, "Porcelain Bodies: Gender, Acquisitiveness, and Taste in Eighteenth-Century England," in John Potvin and Alla Myzelev (eds), *Material Cultures, 1740-1920: The Meanings and Pleasures of Collecting* (Aldershot, UK, and Burlington, VT: Ashgate, 2009), 19–36. See also Eric Weichel, "'Every other Place it could be Placed with Advantage': Ladies-in-waiting at the British Court and the 'Excessive' Display of Ceramics as Art Objects, 1689-1740," in Skelly (ed.), *The Uses of Excess in Visual and Material Culture, 1600-2010*, 41–61.

82   Cheng, *Second Skin*, 150.

83   Ibid., 152.

84   For more on decadence and Orientalism, see Hema Chari, "Imperial Dependence, Addiction, and the Decadent Body," in Constable, Denisoff, and Potolsky (eds), *Perennial Decay: On the Aesthetics and Politics of Decadence*, 215–32.

85   Stacey Sloboda, *Chinoiserie: Commerce and Critical Ornament in Eighteenth-Century Britain* (Manchester and New York: Manchester University Press, 2014), 111.

86   Ibid., 116. See also David Porter, "Monstrous Beauty: Eighteenth-Century Fashion and the Aesthetics of Chinese Taste," *Eighteenth-Century Studies* 35, no. 3 (2002): 395–411.

87   Charmaine A. Nelson, *The Color of Stone: Sculpting the Black Female Subject in Nineteenth-Century America* (Minneapolis and London: University of Minnesota Press, 2007), 57.

88   Ibid., 59.

89   Ibid., 68.

90   Cheng, *Second Skin*, 168.

91   Marcus Wood, "John Gabriel Stedman, William Blake, Francesco Bartolozzi and Empathetic Pornography in the *Narrative of a Five Years Expedition against the Revolted Negroes of Surinam*," in Geoff Quilley and Kay Dian Kriz (eds), *An Economy of Colour: Visual Culture and the Atlantic World, 1660-1830* (Manchester and New York: Manchester University Press, 2003), 129–49.

92   See, for instance, Gilman, "The Hottentot and the Prostitute," 121–6.

93   Charmaine Nelson, *Representing the Black Female Subject in Western Art* (New York and London: Routledge, 2010), 6.

94   Petrine Archer-Straw, *Negrophilia: Avant-Garde Paris and Black Culture in the 1920s* (New York: Thames & Hudson, 2000). For a discussion that addresses the uses of decadence in relation to queer identities in the American context, see Fiona I. B. Ngô, *Imperial Blues: Geographies of Race and Sex in Jazz Age New York* (Durham, NC, and London: Duke University Press, 2014), 89.

95   Cheng, *Second Skin*, 39.

96   Ibid., 121.

97   Ibid., 63.

98   Bernheimer, "Fetishism and Decadence," 82.

99   Ibid., 75.

100 Hamlyn, "Freud, Fabric, Fetish," 22.

3

BAD WOMEN? TRACEY EMIN, GHADA AMER, AND ALLYSON MITCHELL

Bad Girls and *Femmes Fatales*

The figure of the "bad girl" has often been associated with self-destructive behaviors related to consumption and excess. In this way, she is related to the femme fatale of the late nineteenth century, as well as to twentieth-century cinematic versions, in that she is perceived as a threat not only to men but to herself, primarily through acts of excess, whether in terms of alcohol, drugs, sex, or power. In her catalogue essay for the exhibition *Femme Fatale: The Female Criminal*, which was on display at the Justice & Police Museum in Sydney, Australia (2009–10), Nerida Campbell identifies drug addiction as one of the traits of the femme fatale in film and literature. She comments that these "women are independent and thrive outside the boundaries society places around 'good' girls. Some theorists argue the dominance of the femme fatale character during this period directly relates to societal disquiet over the blurring of traditional gender roles caused by World War II."[1]

As Rita Felski has remarked in her discussion of the consuming woman in late-nineteenth- and early-twentieth-century literature and culture, "The familiar and still prevalent cliché of the insatiable female shopper epitomizes the close associations between economic and erotic excess in dominant images of femininity."[2] She identifies the prostitute and the actress as two key female figures during this period because they were both sellers and commodities: "Positioned on the margins of respectable society, yet graphically embodying its structuring logic of commodity aesthetics, the prostitute and the actress fascinated nineteenth-century cultural critics preoccupied with the decadent and artificial nature of modern life."[3] Felski continues:

> One of the most significant features of the expansion of consumption from a feminist standpoint is its preoccupation with women's pleasure. The discourse of consumerism is to a large extent the discourse of female desire. Whereas female sexuality remained a problematic notion throughout the century, its existence either denied or projected onto the deviant figure of the femme fatale, women's desire for commodities could be publicly acknowledged as a legitimate, if often trivialized, form of wanting.[4]

A range of female figures have been framed as threatening because of their consumption, including the femme fatale, the witch, the fat woman, the feminist, the New Woman, and the grotesque woman, which Kate Chedgzoy has theorized in relation to Frida Kahlo's self-portraits, arguing that "Kahlo's paintings of birth, miscarriage, and the grotesque and suffering body, actually represent the process by which the female body is socialized, rendered abject by the technological gaze of patriarchal culture."[5]

Art historian Gill Perry has observed: "Artists such as Tracey Emin, Sarah Lucas and Fiona Banner, whose work draws on popular culture and deploys readable strategies of irony and sexual provocation, have been seen by some to be carrying the torch for a transgressive 'bad girl' art, indulging in an aesthetics of excess." Perry notes that her inspiration for the use of the term "bad girl" was the 1994 *Bad Girls* exhibition at the New Museum of Contemporary Art in New York.[6] The curators of that exhibition identified "excess" as an important trait of so-called "bad girl" artists. Marcia Tanner, one of the curators for the *Bad Girls* exhibition, cites critic Eileen Myles as stating that women are "inherently excessive and outside the law."[7] In a similar vein, Tanya Mars and Johanna Householder have argued: "If the quality associated with Good Girls is control, then the quality most explicitly associated with Bad Girls is excess."[8]

I acknowledge that "bad girls"[9] as a descriptor for feminist artists leaves something to be desired, just as Rozsika Parker and Griselda Pollock pointed out that the phrase "Old Mistresses," the feminine version of Old Masters, is insufficient because of the gendered and sexed significations of the term "mistress."[10] Rather than arguing that the three artists examined in this chapter are "bad girls," I want to show how this phrase has been used to deal with art that is perceived as threatening because it speaks of ostensible female excesses; as noted above, this has sometimes been the response to the work of Tracey Emin, for instance. Further to this, I want to suggest that although the label "bad girls" has unproductive and problematic connotations, I use the phrase "crafty bad girls" with the intention of showing how the artists discussed in this chapter are self-reflexively engaging with beliefs about what makes a woman "bad" as well as what makes art "bad," or, more accurately, *not* art. In other words, like in the previous chapter, I discuss the materials that these artists have chosen as both deliberately "excessive" and "bad" within the context of the art/craft hierarchy, thereby positioning these artworks as "bad objects," to use Naomi Schor's phrase.[11]

I remain ambivalent, however, about my use of the term "bad girl" in this chapter. Marcia Tucker, the other *Bad Girls* curator, may have been too, as she noted that "it took 25 years for grown women to convince men that their use of the term 'girl' was unacceptable to them, but by now the word again has positive connotations in certain circumstances."[12] She goes on to write:

> In the visual arts, increasing numbers of women artists, photographers, cartoonists, performers, video and filmmakers are defying the conventions and proprieties of traditional femininity to define themselves according to their own terms, their own pleasures, their own interests, in their own way. But they're doing it by using a delicious and outrageous sense of humor to make sure not only that everyone gets it, but to really give it to them as well. That's what we mean by "bad girls."[13]

I was hesitant to reuse the phrase "bad girls" in this chapter, even if it was done self-reflexively and with the added prefix of "crafty" to signify strategic, subversive uses of materials and techniques traditionally associated with craft. The alternative, "bad women," does not currently have the same kind of transgressive significations as "bad girl," but it does underscore something that I have been arguing throughout *Radical Decadence*, namely, that women who are perceived as "excessive," whether because of acts of consumption or because they exceed gendered norms, are, as Jack Halberstam has suggested, "failed" women. Put another way, they are "bad women," and Halberstam argues that this identity as failed or "bad" woman can be liberating.[14]

The artists discussed in this chapter exceed a range of gendered stereotypes, such as the silent, docile woman. They are political; they are vocal; they have taken up space with both their bodies and their art. As Mary Russo has remarked:

Reclaiming space has been a central metaphorical concern of modernism and liberation discourse, including women's liberation where it is often understood as a freedom from oppressive bodily containment. I have tried to suggest, thus far, that there may be affirmative models of risk and deviance in the high registers of modernism, and ways in which the image of freedom as limitless space, transcendence, individualism, and upward mobility of various kinds may be embodied and diverted, giving way to a model of feminist practice.[15]

Tracey Emin, Ghada Amer, and Allyson Mitchell have created work that addresses, and grapples with, racism and sexism and homophobia. One could argue that these artists are "bad women," whether they identify as feminist (Amer, Mitchell) or not (Emin). It is also worth noting that even if the term "decadent" is not regularly used in the scholarship written about these artists, the terms "radical" and "excess" appear again and again.[16] With this in mind, I look closely at some of the art criticism that has been written about these artists in order to tease out the insidious stereotypes related to both craft and the "excessive" woman (as well as the "woman artist") that continue to circulate.

There continue to be venomous responses to women who are open about their sexuality and desire for pleasure, and this kind of discourse is one of the primary motivations behind *Radical Decadence*, and indeed one of the axes upon which the book is positioned. It is my objective to critically examine the varied ways in which contemporary feminist artists working with textiles, among other materials, are producing art *despite* this ongoing proscription of female desire and pleasure, as well as ongoing proscriptions regarding the use of fiber in contemporary (feminist) art. In spite of deeply entrenched stigmas related to women's pleasure, some artists persist in representing, or alluding to, female pleasure. As I have set out to demonstrate in previous chapters, one of the primary—if not *the* primary—link between craft, textiles, baked goods, drugs, sex, and consumption more generally is *pleasure through repetition*. As we will see in the section on Ghada Amer, repetition is still perceived as one of the reasons that craft and textile art are regarded as inferior to art that does not employ craft materials or techniques. The chapter is divided into three sections, each dedicated to an individual artist. I begin with British artist Tracey Emin and Egyptian artist Ghada Amer (formerly of Paris, now based in New York), who

Figure 3.1 Ghada Amer, *The Flâneuses*, 2008. Acrylic, embroidery, and gel medium on canvas. 66 × 69 in. (167.6 × 175.3 cm).

were born in the same year (1963), and conclude with Canadian artist Allyson Mitchell and her lesbian lady sasquatches.

To my mind, "bad women" do things *despite* taboos, risks, proscriptions, and prohibitions, whether it means taking drugs, eating "too much," or having "too much" sex, thereby taking the risk of being called a "slut," an experience that Tracey Emin has alluded to in one of her appliqué blankets. It can also mean using textiles and craft techniques in one's art.[17] All of the artists discussed in this chapter, and in *Radical Decadence* as a whole, are aware of these hierarchical divisions between craft and art, and have chosen craft-related materials and techniques not only in spite of this outdated hierarchy, but also because of it. I discuss deliberate failure, amateurism, and "sloppy craft" in the section dedicated to Emin's work. The idea of failure haunted me as I wrote this book, both my own (in securing a tenure-track position), and those failures that (feminist) artists address in their work through and with the use of craft materials. To be a bad girl, or a bad woman, is fundamentally to be a failed woman. The artists in this chapter address that concept in a range of different ways.

Queer theorist Sara Ahmed has argued that "feminists, by declaring themselves feminists, are already read as destroying something that is thought of by others not only as being good but as the cause of happiness. The feminist killjoy spoils the happiness of others; she is a spoilsport because she refuses to convene, to assemble, or to meet up over happiness. In the thick sociality of everyday spaces, feminists are thus attributed as the origin of bad feelings."[18] Although Emin does not identify as feminist, her works have sometimes been read as feminist, in part because of the materials she employs, but also because she engages with the bad feelings that she has experienced as a woman, because she is a woman, and in turn, she has been criticized for bringing others' bad feelings to the surface. Despite her ambivalence about the term "feminist," Emin's work can be productively read through the feminist lens of radical decadence, because in (re)presenting herself as a woman who consumes, she has provoked art criticism that exposes ongoing, insidious beliefs about female drinkers, women who talk about themselves and their emotions (and are consequently labeled as either hysterical or narcissistic), as well as about what a woman artist should or should not do.

Tracey Emin: The art of "self-destruction"

"No artist has so far accomplished his [sic] own self-destruction."[19]

Rozsika Parker wrote in the introduction to the revised edition of *The Subversive Stitch* (2010): "Like nineteen-seventies feminists, Emin employs traditional sampler technique with the incorporation of words."[20] These words are often sexualized, reappropriated slurs against women—for instance, "Pysco [sic] slut" from an appliquéd blanket of 1999—but also allude to the consumption of addictive substances as in her textile work *When I Think About Sex* (2005), which is stitched with the word "Drunk." Parker also alludes to Emin's embroidered tent *Everyone I Have Ever Slept With 1963-1995* (1995), upon which the artist sewed all the names of the people (and teddy bears) that she had slept with up to that point. This work, as well as her installation work *My Bed* (1998), which incorporates dirty linens, challenges the notion of what can be considered a textile artwork.

Emin produced her first appliqué blanket, *Hotel International*, in 1993. According to Neil Brown, "Emin's blankets are also similar to the kinds of banners used in religious, civic or political processions; cathedral banners; trade-union banners; or the banners used on demonstrations and peace protests."[21] There is also an important feminist lineage of banner-use. Brown comments that "women were unlikely to feature among the heroes depicted on trade-union banners, unless winged as angels, or as symbols of virtue."[22] He does not mention suffrage or temperance banners, which were often handmade by women and carried by women, and, in fact, many suffrage banners did represent women as heroines. Lisa Tickner has discussed heroine suffrage banners, which depicted famous women such as Joan of Arc and Boadicea.[23]

Brown observes that "Emin strongly acknowledges her working-class background, but she has emphatically distanced herself from feminism, rejecting discussion of it in her many interviews—other than to acknowledge the endeavours of 1970s feminists. As much as she has resisted it, though, it returns again and again in commentaries of her work, the critical will to consider Emin with feminism's historical or social tendencies seemingly an irresistible force."[24] I would not go so far as to say it is an irresistible force that compels me to discuss Emin's textile works in a book concerned with feminist art, and while Emin may not consider herself a feminist, it is nonetheless productive to consider her work through the feminist framework of radical decadence. As Alexandra Kokoli has written, "Emin's relationship with feminism is famously complicated and deeply ambivalent. The persistence of connecting threads between art and life may be read as ultimately individualist, but cannot help touching on class, race, gender, and sexuality in the context of late twentieth-century Britishness. Like [Judy] Chicago, Emin views her life story as intrinsically significant not just to herself but to other people, especially women."[25]

Emin's biography, as well as her art, is replete with ostensible excesses, not only in terms of emotions (the "emotional" or "hysterical" woman has long been deemed excessive. As Mary Russo has noted, this kind of woman is often perceived as making "a spectacle of herself"), but also in relation to sex (she has had it!) and addictive substances, specifically cigarettes and alcohol, as Gill Perry notes in her discussion of the female contingent of the Young British Artists quoted at the outset of this chapter. If anything, it *is* an irresistible force that compels me to discuss Emin's work in a book about ostensible excesses related to women's consumption and pleasure, and how women artists have engaged with experiences of excess that are often deemed self-destructive.

The art criticism that has been written about Emin's work is notable for reifying certain ideas about "excessive" women. Patrick Elliott has remarked that Emin's

> hectoring blanket texts, which seem to address each viewer individually and directly, are part of our culture. Emin has done this through a very hard-won route. She has a theme, which is nothing other than herself: her body, her life, her problems, her family and friends, her ego and her victories and failures. There is an ancient symbol called the Ouroboros, which shows a snake in the form of a circle, eating its own tail in a process of constant self-renewal. It symbolises infinity or self-sufficiency, but it also captures the nature of Emin's art in that she feeds vicariously upon herself. Her life begets art and her art begets life.[26]

We will recall from the previous chapter that Canadian artist Shary Boyle has produced a ceramic work entitled *Ouroboros* (Plate 9), depicting a red-haired woman whose multiple heads are connected to create a circle, with the final head performing oral sex on the woman: the ultimate in self-sufficiency; indeed, as Elliott says of Emin, the red-headed woman "feeds vicariously upon herself." For Emin, this reading suggests another kind of eating one's self out: of feeding upon both her pain and pleasure to create art. Elliott's statement implies that Emin's life is a kind of performance art. He also frames her as a consuming woman, and like all consuming women, she has been framed as excessive.

Form and content are, in Emin's appliqué blankets, in dialogue, one which speaks eloquently of the intersecting discourses related both to the "excessiveness" of textiles and women's (ostensible) excesses. Janice Helland and Bridget Elliott observe that

> the gendered conflation of textiles—particularly embroidery—with the feminine suggest that somewhere within the softness of fabric and the intricacy of stitching lies an inherent relationship that cannot be signified or secured: it is always "excess" and therefore external to more easily and rigorously defined concepts. Excess is elusive, defies categorization and thus, according to psychoanalytic theorists like Luce Irigaray or Julia Kristeva, occupies the margins, but, particularly following Kristeva, it is precisely in this marginal space that disruption ferments, always ready to dislodge the symbolic order and its dominant discourses.[27]

Rather than reading Emin's blankets as "hectoring" or as heckling the viewer, texts such as "pysco [sic] slut" suggest, on the contrary, that these are phrases that have been used against Emin herself. She is certainly no stranger to cruel words.

In his book *Lucky Kunst: The Rise and Fall of Young British Art* (2009), Gregor Muir writes:

> By the late Nineties, an image had been constructed in the media of the quintessential YBA, largely defined by the antics of the Chapman brothers, Tracey Emin, Damien Hirst and Sarah Lucas, among others. To be a Young British Artist was to be ascribed the following attributes. A "fuck you" attitude was essential, as was drinking excessive amounts of alcohol. Ideally, you had a working-class background and swore a lot. . . . You would appear drunk on television. . . . Constantly flying around the world, you'd stay in the best hotels and trash your room within seconds, leaving a trail of empty vodka bottles and suspiciously smeared mirrors. Whether it was true or not, the relentless media hype began to tar the YBAs. It didn't take long before people wanted to distance themselves from the excess.[28]

The most famous instance of a yBa artist appearing drunk on television was Emin's contribution to a panel entitled "Is Painting Dead?" that took place the night the Turner Prize was awarded in 1997. Gillian Wearing—who, ironically, created a video artwork entitled *Drunk* (1997–99)—won the prize that year.[29] Significantly, art historian David Hopkins has referred to "the spectacle of Tracey Emin drunkenly storming out of an earnest Channel 4 television discussion," affirming Mary Russo's suggestion that "making a spectacle of oneself" is a particularly "feminine danger."[30] Gill Perry has commented: "The crude courting of media notoriety and celebrity status, the strategic deployment of popular culture, resistance to theory, political emptiness and juvenile superficiality have been identified in the works of yBas such as Emin and Lucas, [Sam] Taylor-Wood and Wearing and critiqued by [Julian] Stallabrass, among others. Strategies deployed by such artists have generated a fertile debate on the critical potential of representing excessive behaviour within art practices."[31] I want to consider the ways in which Emin's use of textiles has become inextricably linked with ostensibly "excessive behaviours" including alcohol consumption. Emin has deliberately combined textiles and alcohol in her work more than once. *My Bed*, after all, includes that "trail of empty vodka bottles" to which Muir refers, and she has produced an appliqué blanket entitled *Drunk to the Bottom of My Soul* (2002, private collection). Rather than avoiding the stigmas attached to textiles and the drinking woman, then, Emin has produced work that engages with those very stigmas.

In so doing, Emin highlights her lived experiences of felt emotion; many of her artworks embody what Ann Cvetkovich calls "public feeling."[32] Further to this, Emin presents herself in her work—even when her body is not visible in the image or object—as the grotesque woman who exceeds social norms related to emotionality and "excessive" behavior. She has often been called "Mad Tracey from Margate,"[33] which is also the title of one of her appliqué blankets (1997, Sammlung Goetz, Munich). This moniker, like "pysco [sic] slut," is not insignificant in light of discourses revolving around "the female malady"[34] of hysteria in the nineteenth century, and more recent discourses of the excessively emotional woman whose feelings spill over, rendering her grotesque in the sense of Russo's "grotesque woman" who makes a spectacle of herself in the public sphere.[35] Kate Zambreno, in her book *Heroines* (2012), writes of the "threat of the femme fatale lingering through modernist texts. All the dark ladies of 'The Waste Land,' wounding the impotent Fisher King. She is an excessive, castrating presence, threatening to sweep the subject up into sudden hysteria. . . . A DeKooning horror: FEMME."[36] It is significant that Zambreno cites de Kooning here, as at least one of Ghada Amer's embroidered paintings of porno princesses appears to echo the castrating grin of de Kooning's *Woman* series (Figure 3.1). So, while I do not wish to reentrench the image of Emin as an out-of-control woman who drinks and fucks to excess, it is true that she is playing with the very discourses that would frame her *as* excessive. That she combines this discursive play with textile materials and techniques makes her not only a bad girl (or bad woman), but also a crafty bad girl in both senses of the word "crafty." I want to return to Ahmed briefly in order to cite her textile metaphor regarding "cultural objects" and unhappiness, or other "bad feelings." According to Ahmed, "An unhappy archive is one assembled around the struggle against happiness. We can follow different weaves of unhappiness as a kind of unraveling of happiness and the threads of its appeal."[37] I propose that Emin's work, including the appliqué blankets, *Tent* and *My Bed*, would fit productively in this "unhappy archive."

Take *My Bed*, for instance. Here is a woman's bed, in shambles, surrounded by cigarette boxes, condoms, birth control pills, lubricants, and empty vodka bottles, among other detritus.[38] This is not a "textile" as such, but its employment of bed linens—like Orly Cogan's cocaine and cupcake vintage textile works discussed in the first two chapters— make it a darkly ironic take on the domestic bed that is neither matrimonial nor "safe," even if safe sex is being practiced. In one version of the installation, a noose hung over the bed, adding suicidal overtones.[39] As Neil Brown asserts: "The sheets of *My Bed* are . . . revulsive, and an insult to the idea of a value of grace and harmony that drapery has commanded in art since classical antiquity."[40]

Although *My Bed* is not a textile work that exhibits a pattern as a patchwork quilt might, the word "pattern" can also connote a series of life choices (usually regarded as negative choices) that become a "habit," a word that is sometimes used to describe a person's alcohol or drug use. Indeed, feminist and queer theorist Eve Kosofsky Sedgwick has proposed "habit" as an alternative to "addiction." Sedgwick remarks:

> I'll just suggest briefly that the best luck I've had so far in reconstructing an "otherwise" for addiction attribution has been through a tradition that is, not opposed to it or explanatory of it, but rather one step to the side of it. That is the tradition of reflecting on *habit*, a version of repeated action that moves, not toward metaphysical absolutes, but toward interrelations of the action—and the self acting—with the bodily habitus, the appareling habit, the sheltering habitation, everything that marks the traces of that habit on a world that the metaphysical absolutes would have left a vacuum.[41]

Ann Cvetkovich has also discussed "habits," speaking of the "art of everyday living" and the "utopia of everyday habit" as an antidote for depression. Emin's *My Bed* is a captured moment in her life; it is one representation of the "art of everyday living," or put another way, it depicts "the art of self-destruction." This is one of the veiled, though obvious, facts that Emin illuminates with her work, namely that some women engage in self-destructive behaviors, despite the risks, despite the taboos. These behaviors may evolve into a pattern or a habit, and they may become part of a woman's everyday life.

Artist Julian Schnabel observes regarding Emin's work: "Paint becomes menstrual blood and body fluids and bleating cries of muffled marks and leftover marks and stains and traces that don't let us escape the violence that God and Gravity have laid on us."[42] We will recall Jenni Sorkin's discussion of stains on clothes and other textiles from the previous chapter, in which I examined Nava Lubelski's tablecloth work *Clumsy* (Plate 5). Sorkin examines the symbolic power of stains that also underscores the etymological relationship between being "stained" and being "tainted."[43] Stains are part of *My Bed*; they are intrinsic to it as a work that speaks of patterns or habits.[44] As anthropologist Mary Douglas has stated:

Granted that disorder spoils pattern, it also provides the material of pattern. Order implies restriction; from all possible materials, a limited selection has been made and from all possible relations a limited set has been used. So disorder by implication is unlimited, no pattern has been realised in it, but its potential for patterns is indefinite. This is why, though we seek to create order, we do not simply condemn disorder. We recognise that it is destructive to existing patterns; also that it has potentiality. It symbolises both danger and power.[45]

This anthropological perspective on patterning and the disorder that disrupts, as indicative of both danger and power, illuminates, in part, why Emin's work, and *My Bed* in particular, has caused so much distress among the art-viewing public. It is not as simple as saying that good girls make their beds, while bad girls *don't* make their beds, have lots of sex, and then turn their disheveled bed, stains and all, into Turner-nominated art. This is part of Emin's status as a bad girl artist, yes, granted, but it is not all of it. What is important here, I think, is that despite the taboos related to female sexuality, female excretions, female abjectness, female emotions and emotionality, *and* despite historical degradation of both the consuming woman and women's labor (whether stitching, child-rearing, or homemaking), Emin uses it all to make art. She does not hide in shame. She has refused to hide.

It is worthwhile to quote Emin's own words about the inspiration for *My Bed*. According to Emin, after a week of heavy drinking,

I woke up [and] I was so dehydrated I thought if I don't drink some water I'm going to die. I sort of fell over and crawled my way to the kitchen, got a drink, slowly had a few sips and made my way back to the bedroom, and I stood, and it was like ugh. . . . It was disgusting. And I looked at the bed and thought "Oh my God, I could have died in there" and that's how I would have been found. And then from one second looking horrible it suddenly transformed itself into something removed from me, something outside of me, and something beautiful. I suddenly imagined it out of that context, frozen, outside of my head, in another place.[46]

Neil Brown's analysis of *My Bed* is also worth quoting at length not only because he highlights, without dismissing them as reprehensible, the suggestions of self-destructive tendencies (or patterns) as part of the lived experience of some women, but also because he creates a link between Emin's refusal to bow to proscriptions and Oscar Wilde's downfall due to proscriptions related to sex, consumption, and excess.[47] According to Brown:

> The gross insults to the proper order of things include . . . alcoholism (especially female alcoholism), . . . [and] hormonal hysteria. . . . The stigma that attaches to Emin for these transgressions is greater for her being a female who has chosen to ignore prohibitions against disreputability. In the same way that soiled bed sheets were central evidence in Oscar Wilde's trial (and, after his conviction, his further humiliation through accusations that his sheets in Reading Gaol were stained by masturbation), so Emin is self placed within what is almost a tradition of evidential sexual prejudice. *My Bed* is a work that, just like Victorian painting, features a fallen woman, but where, in this instance, judgmentalism is subverted. For the artist, it is spiritual despair and existential crisis, rather than moral failing, that are the issue, and it is assumed that there is value in the work almost because of, rather than despite, its quality of personal damage.[48]

For all my hesitation about focusing on Emin's life, I would be remiss if I did not underscore Emin's entanglements with sex, alcohol, and other modes of consumption as the very kind of radical decadence that is the heart blood of this book. It is drinking and having sex and using textiles and drugs *in spite* of taboos that have led Emin to be described as a bad girl artist.

Part of the feminist project continues to be the critical examination and deconstruction of scholarship and criticism written about women artists, whether they identify as feminist or not. According to Kokoli, "An important commonality between Emin and Chicago . . . is the widespread hostility and even outright dismissal by which their work has been critically received."[49] Kokoli asserts that both are often identified as "bad" artists, because of their "perceived formal shortcomings," as well as the content of their work, which draws on their own lives and is therefore regarded as confessional, embarrassing, and earnest. Is this not the simplest and, perhaps, most effective, attack on "bad girl" artists? Get rid of the "girl" and you're left with the woman who is, simply, a bad artist. Of course, it is also not insignificant that both Emin and Chicago work with materials that have traditionally been linked with craft and women's (amateur) work.

Negative criticism of Emin has, as we saw in the passage from Muir's *Lucky Kunst*, usually revolved around her ostensible excessiveness: not only her alcohol consumption and sex life—the word "promiscuous" gets thrown around—but also, as I have discussed, her apparent emotionality. As Neil Brown has remarked, "Such an emphatic declaiming of her personal emotions has brought about complaints of exhibitionism and the ego-specific nature of her art."[50] Accusations of "over-sharing" and "too-much-information" are frequently employed to silence the excessive, emotional woman who is related to both Russo's "grotesque woman" and the female hysteric of the nineteenth century. There has also been backlash against Emin's identity as an artist-celebrity, friend to people like

Kate Moss and Madonna, and a woman who has—it is suggested—deliberately catered to the tabloid media with both her "confessional" art and her alleged rock star lifestyle. "Confessional," of course, is a term that had previously been used to describe the poetry of (usually female) poets, such as Sylvia Plath and Anne Sexton, women whose art and lives were perceived as inextricably melded. The fact that both women committed suicide cemented this art/biography knot. Emin, who has referenced her two abortions, among other things, in her art, has been called "confessional" in a way that connects her with the legacy of "tragic" female artists and writers, although Emin is still alive and kicking, now creating work more concerned with the aging female body than with alcohol consumption, which challenges readings of her earlier works as (simply) signifiers of self-destruction. Despite ongoing discourses that expect female drinkers (and drug users) to be punished, morally if not legally, Emin lives on and continues to produce art.[51] She did not die of her "excesses" as a Young British Artist, thereby deflating the image of Emin as powerless over her self-destructive tendencies. Much of the criticism of her art has focused on the "personal" or biographical aspects of her art, and while she has referenced her life in works that do not employ textile materials, such as her drawings, it is not insignificant that Emin has often used craft materials and techniques to produce work that is described as "confessional" and "*faux* amateur," among other things, thereby linking her not only with poets such as Plath and Sexton, but also with women of earlier eras who produced textiles that recorded lived experiences such as births, deaths, imprisonment, and, for some suffragettes, forced feeding.[52]

Craft historian Glenn Adamson describes Emin's oeuvre as a "fabricated and consciously maintained cliché composed of intimate biographical details, explicit sexual confessions, and above all, the constant revelation of the artist's body,"[53] despite the fact that her body is conspicuously *absent* in *Tent*, *My Bed*, and all of her appliqué blankets. Like unworn clothes, these textiles signify the absent female body: the empty space inside the tent, the dent in the pillows, the flatness of the blankets. It is this absence of Emin's body in these textile works that is one of the major differences between her art and the work of second-wave feminist artists who employed their bodies as their medium, although Emin has also frequently represented her body in drawings and photographs.[54]

Adamson also observes that Emin occupies a "*faux* amateur position. . . . Emin's work maps tales of personal rejection through marginalized craft language. So much is clear from her most famous work, *Everyone I Have Ever Slept With, 1963-1995* (1995), a tent with the names of Emin's sleeping partners (both sexual and Platonic) appliquéd to the interior, or the seemingly unending series of quilts, furniture and bags that she has embroidered with a welter of personal slogans and motifs."[55] Although Emin is a trained and professional artist, in appliqué blankets such as *Pysco Slut*, she stitches asymmetrical blocks of fabric to the blanket, resulting in a mishmash of colors, forms, and lettering. I believe that this is what Adamson is referring to when he describes Emin's "*faux* amateur position." Importantly, feminist art historian Kristina Huneault has written convincingly of the discursive work that the term "amateur" has done to degrade women artists, namely justifying their erasure from Western art history.[56] Emin's so-called "amateur position," if she is occupying such a position, is just an act or a pose, to use a Wildean term. It is deliberate, just as the misspelling of "psyco" in the title of *Psyco Slut* is deliberate and intentional, perhaps referencing some of her critics who would sling sexually loaded slurs at her like so much mud. As Alexandra Kokoli points out, the "spelling idiosyncrasies" on Emin's appliqué blankets often result in evocative and resonant puns and double entendres that are rarely commented on in the criticism.[57] So, for instance, when I write the title of Emin's blanket as "psyco [*sic*] slut," the phrase doubles down on framing this invisible female subject as being both mentally ill and sexually promiscuous: a psycho, sick slut.

Emin's deliberately flawed—or deliberately *failed*—appliqué blankets are pointing not only to the slings and arrows that have been directed toward her, but also to the histories of amateur craft produced by women. Joseph McBrinn observes that "feminist artists have long sought to reclaim and reinvest in feminine subjectivity through exploration of this history of exploitative sloppy amateurism and its degradation of women, women's labor, and women's skills."[58] Some artists and scholars, however, have underscored the subversive, even radical, nature of women's amateur crafting. Lou Cabeen writes:

In the language of Arts and Crafts advocates . . . the roles of artist, who produces an original image, and artisan, who fabricates it, have not fused into the same worker, but have stayed separate. In that view, the labor of the home embroiderer working a commercially produced pattern is trivial and alienated. *Historically, the arts have taught us to see this as failure*, a cop out for the artisan and a loss of control for the artist. This hierarchy based on a narrow definition of originality continues to inform much contemporary discourse, leading to labels that distinguish between the relative merits of the labor involved in "art," "craft," "hobby," and "kitsch."[59]

Emin's deliberate flaws, or failures, in her appliqué blankets illuminate the intersecting histories of amateur crafting, women's labor, and the specter of the failed woman. Her work, which could perhaps be described as "sloppy craft,"[60] engages with ideologies related not only to materiality, textiles, and art, but also to gendered ideologies that continue to circulate about women, expectations, roles, excess, and (ostensible) perfection. Elaine C. Paterson and Susan Surette describe sloppy craft as "a consciously deskilled aesthetic," that is, a *deliberate* failure in skill and craftsmanship.[61] As Sandra Alfoldy observes, "Sloppy craft suggests a purposeful approach to failure. Employing a purposeful approach indicates expertise or professionalism, or the ability to differentiate between good and bad technical skills, which reinforces the idea that the craft artist chooses to work in this way."[62] Emin, through her deliberately failed textile works, positions herself as a failed, or "bad," woman.[63]

In her consideration of the pleasure inherent in craft, Cabeen observes that when she was growing up, her great-grandmother embroidered at home, and on one occasion, Cabeen "entered the silence of my great-grandmother. The steady concentration of her stitching built a shield around us both. Silent and safely occupied, we both—the very young and the very old—became invisible to the middle aged as their harried and perplexing lives swirled around us."[64] Textiles have been used for large-scale battles, as in the case of the late-nineteenth- and early-twentieth-century suffrage movement. For Cabeen's great-grandmother, her stitching was employed as a shield silently and on a small scale. Craft has long been maligned and positioned as inferior to painting. It is partly for this reason that contemporary (feminist) artists who employ craft materials and craft techniques are radical and, indeed, excessive. Their combined choice of materials and their subject matter (so often having to do with pleasure, consumption, and ostensible excess) is what makes them "crafty bad girls" and "bad women."

Ghada Amer: Striking a pose[65]

In the 1992 edition of her edited collection *Pleasure and Danger: Exploring Female Sexuality* (1984, 1992), Carole S. Vance refers to the "threads of increasing sexual pleasure" that have been part of the "rich tapestry" of feminist political action.[66] As we have seen throughout *Radical Decadence*, it is not unusual for feminist theorists and scholars to employ textile metaphors in their discussions of first-wave, second-wave, and third-wave feminism. This is, of course, both significant and unsurprising, considering the close relationships between historical women, textiles, craft, feminism, and recent examples of feminist art, which are, as I have been arguing, both radical and excessive.

Ghada Amer's paintings—which comprise canvas, paint, and threads—combine gendered materials and gendered subject matter (female subjects taken from pornographic magazines) to radically subvert ideologies related to the female body and female sexuality. Amer's work invites a wide range of readings. While a feminist viewer may find her paintings beautiful, even scintillating, arousing, and, by turns, funny, that same feminist viewer may conclude that Amer's paintings are problematic because they do not go far enough in subverting a masculine visual language related to the sexualization of the female body. In what follows, I draw on a number of texts written about Amer's paintings, and I offer my own reading of her work that represents (unhappy) housewives, Disney princesses, and porn stars, or porn princesses, as I will be calling them to underscore their close discursive relationship with Amer's Disney princesses (Figure 3.1), but it goes without saying that this is only one feminist reading among many, and I leave it to the reader to arrive at his or her own conclusions about Amer's oeuvre as a whole.

Amer was born in Cairo in 1963. She studied at the Villa Arson in Nice (1989) and the Institut des hautes études en arts plastiques in Paris (1991), and she is currently based in New York. Both her birthplace and her training have contributed greatly to her choice of subject matter and her primary medium, which is painting, but with thread and embroidery simulating the effects of dripping paint. She has also produced installations, often incorporating text, as well as public art in gardens and streets. Like Mickalene Thomas, she is adamant that her paintings be called paintings, despite the fact that they incorporate craft materials and techniques. For Amer, because painting has long been gendered masculine, while embroidery has been gendered feminine, it is a feminist maneuver to co-opt the word "painting" for works that combine paint and thread. As Maria Elena Buszek remarks: "While her insistence on referring to her embroidered canvases as 'paintings' is a pointed rebellion against a male art professor—in France, not Egypt—who refused to teach women the 'masculine' art of painting, she simultaneously, contradictorily insists on referencing the 'feminine nature' of needlework and fiber arts as no less an act of defiance. She appropriates the image of the sexualized woman as an icon of feminist sexuality, yet she has frequently dismissed her source material as sexist."[67]

Amer began using embroidery in her art around 1990 after she discovered an issue of *Venus*, a fashion magazine for Muslim women, which was dedicated to the veil.[68] In her series *Cinq Femmes au Travail* (*Five Women at Work*) from 1991, the works depict in red thread women engaged in activities such as grocery shopping, vacuuming, baking, and child-carrying. According to Amer, "Rather than represent women in a comfortable environment, I wanted these images to reflect the melancholy of this so-called comfort."[69] The fifth "woman" referred to in the series title is the unrepresented Amer, thus identifying art-making as another form of "woman's work." These works are very simple: against a beige ground (unprimed canvas), the outlines of the women's bodies and props are stitched in red. The tiny knots of thread where Amer has tied off the end of her thread are clearly visible, making the work appear noticeably imperfect, in a way that recalls Emin's imperfect appliqué blankets that are inscribed with poorly spelled words and jagged letters. Both Amer and Emin, it is worth noting, were trained, professional artists when they produced these works. The deliberate imperfection of these textiles is an ironic play with the idea of polished painting versus "amateur" crafting. They are embracing imperfection as part of an artistic project that questions both art-historical hierarchies and ideologies related to female sexuality and creative production. On Emin's appliqué blankets, she sewed phrases such as "pysco [sic] slut," "your [sic] good in bed" (on *Hotel International*, 1993), and the full title of *Mad Tracey from Margate* includes the subtitle, *Everyone's Been There* (1997), implying female promiscuity and accessibility.

Tiring of housewives and domestic activities, in 1992 Amer turned for visual material to heteronormative pornographic magazines intended for the masculine gaze.[70] As Maura Reilly has remarked, "Amer's embroidered porn stars illustrate a tension that has in fact always been present in the traditional models of ideal womanhood. While women on the one hand are trained to become the mother/wife, learning housekeeping and pressured to retain and uphold proper moral values that they will in turn instill in their children, the sexual fantasies of men often desire another kind of woman. The whore/mistress is the wife's inverse, sexually adventurous and available."[71] In this ongoing project, Amer chooses images of women—naked, often masturbating—cuts them out, and transfers them to her canvases, representing them either in paint or with thread. The pornographic women in Amer's works have stitches that have visible gaps between them, making these bodies perforated, permeable, and penetratable, in contrast to the Disney princesses in later works who are inviolate with their solid outlines. Here, then, we have yet another instance of the medium being the message. Male figures are rarely represented, so the paintings are images of women self-pleasuring or engaging in oral sex with other women. Her addition of thread, often in colorful, ejaculatory waterfalls *over* these pornographic bodies, blocks easy visual access to the bodies, for example, in *Pink* (2000; Plate 10) and even more dramatically in *Knotty But Nice* (2005; Plate 11).

From the early 2000s, the bodies began to be more illegible (in part because the threads on the front of the canvases became longer; Amer also sometimes knotted the threads on the front of the canvas instead of the back), suggesting that Amer wanted to make it even harder for the viewer to access the female subjects. This is the case in paintings such as *Red and White Lovers* (2002), *Eight Women in Black and White* (2004), *Heather's Degradé* (2006), and *Scheherazade* (2009), among others. These works are not necessarily antipornography, however. Amer has stated that she chooses images of women from the magazines that she finds sexy, and her work has been read, from a feminist perspective, as concerned with female empowerment via pleasure and desire. In an interview from 2000, Amer proclaimed, in relation to pornography: "I see it as something beautiful and warm, a source of pleasure. Feminism can be empowered by seduction."[72]

In the early 1990s, Amer began to integrate representations of Disney princesses into her work, and eventually alongside the pornographic women.[73] One scholar argues that this uncomfortable juxtaposition highlights the latent sexuality in fairy tales.[74] Amer herself has underscored the various messages that young girls are taught through fairy tales, such as the myth of Prince Charming. Amer's paintings that combine pornographic scenes with Disney princesses speak to the thin line between the princess as an ideal and the female sex worker as a reality. In other words, while (some) young girls turn into women who continue to believe that their Prince Charming is still out there somewhere, the reality is sometimes far more grim. Part of the myth that some Western women seem to keep buying into is that their wedding is an opportunity to be princesses for a day.

In *Les Flâneuses* (Figure 3.1), four female figures fill the canvas, while to the left a woman's head and breast are clearly visible because of the dark outline of her body. She looks out provocatively at the viewer, her teeth bared, recalling Willem de Kooning's *Woman I* (1952, Museum of Modern Art, New York) with its robust, threatening female subject and Abstract Expressionist painterliness, which is simulated in *Les Flâneuses* with both thread and paint drips.[75] To the right of the large female figure with bared teeth is Snow White, who is surrounded by animals, including the bird perched on her finger.[76] Art historian Carol Duncan describes the woman in de Kooning's painting as a "primal mother-whore."[77] In a different essay, she states: "The woman figure had been emerging gradually in de Kooning's work in the course of the 1940s. By 1951–52, it fully revealed itself in *Woman I* as a big, bad mama—vulgar, sexual, and dangerous. De Kooning imagines her facing us with iconic frontality, large, bulging eyes, open, toothy mouth, massive breasts. The suggestive pose is just a knee movement away from open-thighed display of the vagina, the self-exposing gesture of mainstream pornography."[78] In her paintings, Amer gives us much more than suggestive poses; she gives us a myriad of self-exposing gestures, both vaginal and anal, that are appropriated from pornographic magazines for men and recycled in feminist paintings concerned with women's pleasure and desire, and (arguably) women's empowerment.

While I acknowledge that Amer's paintings are subversive in their use of textiles to obscure graphic sexual poses taken from pornographic magazines, I am hesitant to regard these paintings as purely empowering. Amer is appropriating imagery from magazines, and is therefore employing still images, rather than images that she has taken from pornographic films. Nonetheless, pornographic photography is a form of sex work, and there are crucial questions about agency, financial remuneration, and women's embodied labor that are raised, if not addressed, by Amer's paintings. I am mindful of Mellisa Bull's indictment of a society that both stigmatizes and facilitates female prostitution in her preface to Nelly Arcan's *Burqa of Skin*. Arcan, a writer who committed suicide in 2009, worked as an escort while she was studying at university, in all likelihood, in order to afford her education. Bull writes: *"Filles de joie*? Certainly not. Even when their physical well-being is not threatened, women who exert this trade live not in joy but in death, day after day."[79] Bull links prostitution and pornography as two forms of sex work under the phrase "theatre of p&p, the theatre of prostitution and pornography," which, she says, "is frozen in the present, stuck in the immobility of a tableau, of the stage, of the pose, of the position of the 'rhetorical figure'. It stops time and isolates the individual, and thus lends itself admirably to nihilism."[80] Although Amer is not fully antipornography, and, indeed, one of the reasons that radical feminism lost favor was the antipornography stance promulgated by some radical feminists,[81] there will inevitably be different feminist responses to Amer's paintings that depict pornographic poses.

What makes Amer's work "excessive"? As with the other artists discussed in *Radical Decadence* so far, it is both her medium and her subject matter. As Thérèse St-Gelais observes:

> Chromatic quietude is rare in Ghada Amer's work. Her modus operandi is extravagance, excess even, in the sense applied to English romantic painting but also in a transgressive sense, for she deals with subjects that do not readily conform to the rules of art—and in a context, moreover, where pleasure seems to be fully assumed. The lust that fills her works is accompanied by the visual and tactile sensuality of her materials, which strikes us immediately. In fact, it is only when we move closer to a work that we see what is concealed behind the coloured field. Intoxicated by the allure of the *matière*, we realize only subsequently that, in the background, other pleasures are being played out.[82]

Her threads *exceed* the canvas both symbolically and literally, spilling over the bodies of women who are engaged in sexual acts. Many of these women, engaged in masturbation, are, like the woman represented in Boyle's *Ouroboros* (Plate 9), self-pleasuring and self-sufficient. They wait for no man or woman. Although they have been appropriated from men's pornographic magazines, they do not need men to experience pleasure within the pictorial space of Amer's paintings.

As with Emin, criticism of Amer's work, even in ostensibly positive discussions in exhibition catalogues, often illuminates ongoing (perceived) hierarchies related to art and craft, the latter still often associated with pattern, repetition, and femininity. For instance, in a catalogue essay for a 2007 exhibition in Rome, curator Danilo Eccher writes:

> Embroidery is not painting, even if it seems to be; it is difficult to compare it to creative language and it is, instead, a traditional practice, a maniacal and obsessive skill, expanded autistically over time, repetitive work, without emotion, shadowy. Embroidery does not possess an extended, dynamic glance, but rather one that is more fixed, immobile, almost myopic in the rigidity of its stitching. Challenging the inflexibility of this practice to accord it creative language is the risky and subtle feat that Ghada Amer achieves in her art. It is work that accepts the subjugation of time, the maniacal nature of repetition, and the fastidious virtuosity of a somewhat coarse craftsmanship.

The first sentence of this passage is remarkable, considering that Amer has, since the early 1990s, identified her works that employ embroidery as paintings. The insistence by this writer that embroidery is not only a "traditional practice" but also a "maniacal" and "obsessive skill" serves as a one-two punch, albeit one easily dismissed by feminist readers, that explicitly aligns craft with (feminine) madness and excess, a kind of female malady that manifests itself in stitching. Additionally, in referring to embroidery as a "skill," the author buys into the art/craft hierarchy according to which craft is a skill predicated on "obsessive" repetition, rather than an art, which is produced in the realm of individual creative genius. Ironically, the writer repeats himself, when he uses the term "maniacal" a second time to describe embroidery's "nature of repetition." He concludes with a left-handed compliment, namely that Amer "subtly" subverts the "fixed, immobile, almost myopic . . . rigidity of . . . stitching," while still producing what the author calls "the fastidious virtuosity of a somewhat coarse craftsmanship."[83]

Allyson Mitchell, the final artist to be discussed in this chapter, deliberately engages with this kind of outdated (and, perhaps, outgoing) discourse by deliberately, and ironically, choosing craft-related materials that have literally and metaphorically been discarded in the rubbish bin of history. She also engages with discourses related to the ostensible monstrosity of "excessive" lesbian women by creating massive sculptures of lady sasquatches using fun fur and other "kitschy" materials (Plate 12).

Allyson Mitchell: Decadent lesbian monsters

My discussion of Emin's work as part of an "unhappy archive" is indebted to both Sara Ahmed and to Ann Cvetkovich's discussion of Canadian lesbian feminist artist Allyson Mitchell's art as part of Cvetkovich's "depression archive." Whereas Cvetkovich is primarily concerned with the ways that Mitchell's drawings, textiles, and installations function as sites of and for "public feeling," including but not limited to depression, I am more interested in the ways that Mitchell, who describes herself as a "maximalist," and therefore is self-consciously engaging with discourses of excess, can be positioned as a crafty bad girl because of her choice of materials, her subject matter, and her writings on both lesbian feminisms and young feminisms.[84]

According to Cvetkovich,

Mitchell often finds the materials for her art in thrift stores, where she has collected shag rugs, crocheted afghans, ceramic figurines, fake fur, and macramé plant holders. While some versions of crafting reject mass production in favor of handmade or artisanal production, Mitchell's work engages with the marketplace of commodities, but often in its more abject forms. Recycling objects and styles associated with previous generations, Mitchell is drawn to that which has been rejected as outmoded or déclassé (and hence a trigger for deep feelings). For her, the strong and frequently negative feelings attached to objects that are sentimental, cute, garish, cheap, or *excessive* resemble the feelings associated with both fat girls and feminisms, and this reservoir of shame, abjection, and mixed feelings is a resource for queer reparative strategies. Collecting the lost objects that others left behind to be thrown away or sold for cheap, and collecting in massive quantities that reveal consumption's popular trends, she creates new worlds out of discarded ones.[85]

In positioning Mitchell as a crafty bad girl, scholars have identified her work as excessive (in a good way), as well as radical. Various writers have used this word to describe both her lesbian politics and her use of craft materials and techniques. In addition to the long passage quoted above, Cvetkovich has remarked that because "craft produces objects that are both useful and *exceed the necessary*, it is readily available to commodified proliferation, but it is also about art in everyday life."[86] In her "Deep Lez I Statement," Mitchell observes: "Deep Lez uses cafeteria-style mixings of craft, context, food, direct action, and human connections to maintain radical dyke politics and resistant strategies."[87] Throughout this chapter, and throughout *Radical Decadence*, it has become clear that scholars and curators are still using the term "radical" to describe contemporary (feminist) artists' use of craft materials and techniques. Another example is Sarah Quinton's observation that "if Judy Chicago's textile works . . . are considered to be fundamentally feminist expressions, it is not simply the 'radical' suggestion that textiles—a genteel, private and 'female' medium—might qualify as a form of 'capital-A' art in the context of a mainstream public art gallery or museum environment that has caused her work to be met with controversy for being feminist, populist or too sexually illustrative." Rather, Quinton argues, Chicago's "mobilization of tapestry, embroidery and quilting—as well as sculpture and painting—to shape graphic, large-scale and at times discomfiting images . . . interrupted a neatly packaged modernist art-world hegemony with a powerful combination of process and image, tactility and seductiveness."[88] This repeated use of the term "radical" indicates, first, that there are still stigmas attached to craft in the Western art world, but secondly, and more importantly, that craft can still signify as radical because of, rather than in spite of, historical connotations of "femininity" and women's work. For Mitchell, her radical lesbian politics are interwoven with her radical use of craft materials.

It has been noted in various publications that Mitchell identifies Judy Chicago as one of her role models, acknowledging both her use of craft techniques and materials, and her importance for feminist art. This is significant in light of the fact that many feminist critics and artists dismissed Chicago's *The Dinner Party* (Plate 1) for being essentializing and for focusing on "core imagery" (i.e., vaginal imagery) and other second-wave feminist artistic strategies. Mitchell notes that "this criticism had the effect of disarticulating Chicago's work from 'feminism' (or an appropriate feminism), resulting in a breakdown of intergenerational and interpolitical dialogue. The tendency in feminist politics to dismiss or excoriate that which came before at the dawn of new theories and political strategies has dangerous consequences. As Judy Chicago has pointed out, such an approach prevents the development of a feminist history, instead forcing young women to continue to identify with male history."[89]

In addition to recognizing Mitchell's art as both excessive and radical, one could also argue that her work is "decadent" in that it engages with the figure of the "monstrous" woman and lesbian, a figure that was represented in both decadent poetry and art of the late nineteenth century, for instance in decadent poet Charles Baudelaire's *Les Fleurs du Mal* (1857). In his study of nineteenth-century art representing women, Bram Dijkstra observes that "Baudelaire had already subverted the analogy's positive symbolism [woman as flower] by referring to women as flowers of evil, and now the link between the flowers and the earth opened the chasm of sexual hunger between woman and the ideal of her floral inanity."[90] But rather than coping with anxieties about women's increased social and sexual freedom, as decadent male artists were doing by depicting women as threatening and monstrous, Mitchell has created female monsters to make visible the very discourses and beliefs that would frame lesbian women (and "bad" women more generally) as grotesque (Figures 3.2–3.4). According to Cvetkovich, "Mitchell makes large-scale installations, including a series featuring the Ladies Sasquatch, a band of giant lesbian monsters whose overblown size is inspired by Mitchell's fat activism."[91] Mitchell started working on the Ladies Sasquatch project in 2002. Most critics have focused on these installations (it is an ongoing exhibition) as lesbian, or Sapphic, figures, empowered and empowering, kitschy, and "monstrous but domesticated."[92] I agree with Josephine Mills when she writes that the Ladies Sasquatch are "challenging ideals of femininity and heterosexuality, and physically manifesting misogynist fears."[93] Significantly for the discussion of Amer's work in this chapter, Mills also remarks: "The Sasquatches are a visual pun and a manifestation of homophobic fears of actual lesbians. They are big, fat, hairy dykes—the exact opposite of the nubile lesbians of patriarchal porn—the kind of lezzies who wear army boots and are referred to as 'scary'."[94] Mitchell, then, goes beyond direct quotations from pornographic depictions of same-sex desire between women to create larger-than-life lesbian beasts.

Critics have also focused on the importance of (lesbian) community suggested by the Ladies Sasquatch installations, and the possibility of social change via this work, implying a utopia not only of "everyday habits," but of queer agency and queer artistic practice.[95]

Figure 3.2 Allyson Mitchell, detail from exhibition of *Ladies Sasquatch*, 2010. Found textiles, wood, Styrofoam, plastic, glass, fiberglass, and metal. McMaster Museum of Contemporary Art, Hamilton, Ontario. Photograph by Cat O'Neil. Courtesy of the artist.

Figure 3.3 Allyson Mitchell, detail from exhibition of *Ladies Sasquatch*, 2010. Found textiles, wood, Styrofoam, plastic, glass, fiberglass, and metal. McMaster Museum of Contemporary Art, Hamilton, Ontario. Photograph by Cat O'Neil. Courtesy of the artist.

Figure 3.4 Allyson Mitchell, detail from exhibition of *Ladies Sasquatch*, 2010. Found textiles, wood, Styrofoam, plastic, glass, fiberglass, and metal. McMaster Museum of Contemporary Art, Hamilton, Ontario. Photograph by Cat O'Neil. Courtesy of the artist.

The Ladies Sasquatch also parody the preoccupation with artificiality and women's same-sex desire evidenced by male decadent artists and writers at the end of the nineteenth century. Victorian art critics also saw signs of "lesbianism" in works by Pre-Raphaelite artist Edward Burne-Jones, whose work has sometimes been categorized as Symbolist. Octave Mirbeau (1870–1917) commented regarding Burne-Jones's depictions of women: "The rings under their eyes . . . are unique in the whole history of art; it is impossible to tell whether they are the result of masturbation, lesbianism, normal love-making or tuberculosis."[96]

I am not suggesting that Mitchell is deliberately parodying, or even referencing, *fin-de-siècle* decadence. However, her self-reflexive use of artificial materials such as fun fur, and indeed, other "kitschy"[97] or "excessive" materials such as glitter and sequins, speaks to a deliberate dance with ornamental, crafty excess, which Cvetkovich aligns with camp theatricality and glamour.[98] It is also, I want to suggest, a contemporary feminist and queer twist on the artificiality and ornamental excesses celebrated by late-nineteenth-century male decadents. Further to this, as we have seen, both Mitchell and the feminist critics and curators writing about her work see the Ladies Sasquatch as lesbian "monsters," and this echoes the preoccupation not only with the monstrous woman (or femme fatale) but also with the lesbian in *fin-de-siècle* decadent art and writing. It is also worth noting, as discussed in the Introduction to *Radical Decadence*, that Bridget Elliott and Jasmine Rault have considered the importance of decadent aesthetics for early-twentieth-century lesbian (or "non-heterosexual") artists and designers.[99]

As Mills has previously argued, Mitchell's funny, huge, patchwork, sculptural, comforting, and sexual Ladies Sasquatch make manifest the ways that masculine culture has rendered the (lesbian) woman monstrous. It has frequently been noted that late-nineteenth-century male decadent writers were misogynistic. Oscar Wilde is sometimes included in this characterization, although sometimes he is excused. According to Jane Marcus, "Oscar Wilde did not approach women with fear and loathing. He liked strong women."[100] Male artists identified as Symbolists, or Decadents, have also been discussed in terms of misogyny. Charles Bernheimer, for instance, has discussed Gustave Moreau's paintings of Salome in relation to Wilde's play *Salomé* (1891), analyzing the visual and textual representations in terms of castration anxieties and Medusa.[101] He observes: "Castration, fetishism, decadence, the mirror of Medusa—the single fin-de-siècle figure who served to focus the interplay of these factors most dramatically was Salome."[102] He goes on to describe the "decadent vision of Salome as vicious femme fatale" and notes that she is described as "the monstrous Beast" in J. K. Huysmans's decadent novel *A rebours* (1884).[103] Ultimately, Bernheimer argues that "Wilde's gaze, cultivated in the library like a decadent plant in the hothouse, exaggerates to the point of comic absurdity the characteristic traits of the femme fatale."[104] If Wilde's Salome is a comically absurd femme fatale, then Mitchell's Ladies Sasquatch have pushed the envelope even further in turning desiring women, women who desire women, into giant furry beasts. These are lesbians in a "parodic mode." They are literally monstrous and literal monsters. They are perverse sexual "deviants." Bernheimer argues that Aubrey Beardsley evokes "perversity" in his illustrations for Wilde's *Salomé* "in the many suggestions of deviant sexual practices that suffuse the image[s]."[105] The Lady Sasquatches are also certainly failed "ladies" in terms of their bodies, behaviors, and queerness. They are not polite or "nice." They moon their audience, they snarl, they claw. Carla Garnet notes, drawing on Monique Wittig, that to "be a lesbian is a refusal of the 'role' of woman."[106] The Lady Sasquatches are very bad women, though, really, they are not women at all. Some feminist viewers will perceive the Lady Sasquatches as angry, while others will see them, as Hélène Cixous saw Medusa, as laughing.[107] I want to suggest that both anger and laughter are consequences of, and inspirations for, radical decadence as a feminist approach to art and life.

Notes

1   Nerida Campbell (ed.), "Femme Fatale: The Female Criminal," in *Femme Fatale: The Female Criminal* (Sydney: Historic Houses Trust of New South Wales, 2008), 8. See also Mary Ann Doane, *Femmes Fatales: Feminism, Film Theory, Psychoanalysis* (New York and London: Routledge, 1991).

2   Rita Felski, *The Gender of Modernity* (Cambridge, MA, and London: Harvard University Press, 1995), 62.

3   Ibid., 20.

4   Ibid., 64–65.

5   Kate Chedgzoy, "Frida Kahlo's 'Grotesque' Bodies," in P. Florence and D. Reynolds (eds), *Feminist Subjects, Multi-Media: Cultural Methodologies* (Manchester: Manchester University Press, 1995), 48.

6   Gill Perry, "Introduction," in Gill Perry (ed.), *Difference and Excess in Contemporary Art: The Visibility of Women's Practice* (Oxford: Blackwell Publishing, 2004), 5–6.

7   Quoted in Marcia Tanner, "Preface," in Marcia Tanner and Marcia Tucker, *Bad Girls*, exh. cat. (New York: The New Museum of Contemporary Art/Cambridge, MA: The MIT Press, 1994), 10.

8   Tanya Mars and Johanna Householder (eds), *Caught in the Act: An Anthology of Performance Art by Canadian Women* (Toronto: YYZ Books, 2004), 49.

9   See "Who's Bad? A Mixed Response to a Season of Bad Girls," *Frieze,* issue 15 (March/April 1994) http://www.frieze.com/issue/article/whos_bad/(last accessed December 15, 2015). This article comprises several abbreviated reviews of the *Bad Girls* exhibition, which often criticized the simplistic, "trendy" use of "bad girls" as a framework for the exhibition.

10   Rozsika Parker and Griselda Pollock, *Old Mistresses: Women, Art and Ideology* (London: Routledge and Kegan Paul, 1981).

11   Ellen Rooney, "Foreword: An Aesthetic of Bad Objects," in Naomi Schor (ed.), *Reading in Detail: Aesthetics and the Feminine* (1987; New York and London: Routledge, 2007), xiii–xxxv.

12   Marcia Tucker, "Introduction," in Marcia Tanner and Marcia Tucker, *Bad Girls*, exh. cat. (New York: The New Museum of Contemporary Art/Cambridge, MA: The MIT Press, 1994), 4.

13   Ibid., 5.

14   Judith Halberstam, *The Queer Art of Failure* (Durham, NC, and London: Duke University Press, 2011).

15   Mary Russo, *The Female Grotesque: Risk, Excess and Modernity* (New York and London: Routledge, 1994), 26.

16   For a thorough analysis of radical feminism, see Alice Echols, *Daring to Be Bad: Radical Feminism in America 1967-1975* (Minneapolis: University of Minnesota Press, 1989).

17   Jefferies, "Contemporary Textiles," 44.

18   Sara Ahmed, "Killing Joy: Feminism and the History of Happiness," *Signs: Journal of Women in Culture and Society* 35, no. 3 (2010): 581.

19   Jean Gimpel, *Against Art and Artists* (1968; Edinburgh: Polygon, 1991), 143.

20   Rozsika Parker, *The Subversive Stitch: Embroidery and the Making of the Feminine* (1984; London and New York: I. B. Tauris, 2010), xv.

21   Neal Brown, *Tracey Emin* (London: Tate Publishing, 2006), 40.

22 Ibid.

23 Lisa Tickner, *The Spectacle of Women: Imagery of the Suffrage Campaign 1907-14* (London: Chatto & Windus, 1988), 69. See also Parker, *The Subversive Stitch*, 200.

24 Brown, *Tracey Emin*, 40.

25 Alexandra Kokoli, "Sisters," in Rachel Dickson (ed.), *Judy Chicago and Louise Bourgeois, Helen Chadwick, Tracey Emin* (London: Lund Humphries, 2012), 170.

26 Patrick Elliott (ed.), "Becoming Tracey Emin," in *Tracey Emin 20 Years* (Edinburgh: National Galleries of Scotland, 2008), 33.

27 Bridget Elliott and Janice Helland, "Introduction," in Elliott and Helland (eds), *Women Artists and the Decorative Arts, 1880-1935: The Gender of Ornament*, 5.

28 Gregor Muir, *Lucky Kunst: The Rise and Fall of Young British Art* (London: Aurum Press, 2012), 220.

29 Ibid., 215.

30 David Hopkins, "'Out of It': Drunkenness and Ethics in Martha Rosler and Gillian Wearing," in Gill Perry (ed.), *Difference and Excess in Contemporary Art: The Visibility of Women's Practice* (Malden, MA, and Oxford: Blackwell Publishing, 2004), 38. Russo, *The Female Grotesque*, 53.

31 Perry, "Introduction," 6.

32 Ann Cvetkovich, *Depression: A Public Feeling* (Durham, NC, and London: Duke University Press, 2012).

33 "Mad Tracey from Margate" is the title of the chapter on Emin in Muir's *Lucky Kunst*, 213.

34 Elaine Showalter, *The Female Malady: Women, Madness, and English Culture, 1830-1980* (New York: Penguin, 1985).

35 Russo, *The Female Grotesque*, 53.

36 Kate Zambreno, *Heroines* (Los Angeles: Semiotext(e), 2012), 121.

37 Ahmed, "Killing Joy," 573.

38 See Jennifer Doyle, "The Effects of Intimacy: Tracey Emin's Bad-Sex Aesthetics," in Mandy Merck and Chris Townsend (eds), *The Art of Tracey Emin* (London: Thames & Hudson, 2002), 102–18.

39 Deborah Cherry, "On the Move: *My Bed*, 1998-1999," in Merck and Townsend (eds), *The Art of Tracey Emin*, 134–54.

40 Brown, *Tracey Emin*, 100.

41 Eve Kosofsky Sedgwick, "Epidemics of the Will," in *Tendencies* (Durham, NC, and London: Duke University Press, 1993), 138.

42 Julian Schnabel, "The Loneliness of the Long-Distance Runner," in Patrick Elliott (ed.), *Tracey Emin 20 Years*, 12.

43 Jenni Sorkin, "Stain: On Cloth, Stigma, and Shame," in Hemmings (ed.), *The Textile Reader*, 59–63.

44 On textiles and patterns, see Kerstin Kraft, "Textile Patterns and their Epistemological Function," *Textile: The Journal of Cloth and Craft* 3, no. 3 (Autumn 2004): 275–89.

45 Mary Douglas, *Purity and Danger: An Analysis of Concepts of Pollution and Taboo* (1966; New York: Routledge, 2001), 95.

46 "In conversation with Carl Freedman," in Carl Freedman (ed.), *Tracey Emin: Work 1963-2006* (2006), 251–52. Quoted in Elliott, "Becoming Tracey Emin," 29.

47 For more on this, see Julia Skelly (ed.), "The Paradox of Excess: Oscar Wilde, Caricature, and Consumption," in *The Uses of Excess in Visual and Material Culture, 1600–2010* (Farnham, UK and Burlington, VT: Ashgate, 2014), 137–60.

48 Brown, *Tracey Emin*, 102.

49 Kokoli, "Sisters," 173.

50 Brown, *Tracey Emin*, 7.

51 According to Susan Boyd, "In illegal-drug films, women must pay for their drug use, and there is rarely any escape from their destiny: sexual degradation, pregnancy, suicide, and drug overdose accompany women's drug use." Susan C. Boyd, *Hooked: Drug War Films in Britain, Canada, and the United States* (Toronto: University of Toronto Press, 2008), 148.

52 On textiles produced by women to mark a loved one's death, see Maureen Daly Goggin, "Stitching (in) Death: Eighteenth- and Nineteenth-Century American and English Mourning Samplers," in Maureen Daly Goggin and Beth Fowkes Tobin (eds), *Women and the Material Culture of Death* (Farnham, UK, and Burlington, VT: Ashgate, 2013), 63–89. Glenn Adamson discusses an embroidered handkerchief made by suffragette Janie Terrero in Holloway Prison in 1912; she had been arrested for smashing the window of an Oxford Street engineering shop. The handkerchief includes the W.S.P.U.'s motto, "Deeds not Words," at the top, and in the upper-left corner the words "Hunger strike April 13th to 19th" have been embroidered. In the center of the handkerchief are the words "Worked in Holloway Prison by Janie Terrero," thereby negating the belief that women's textiles were never "signed." Glenn Adamson, *The Invention of Craft* (London: Bloomsbury, 2013), 223.

53 Adamson, *Thinking through Craft*, 161.

54 See Amelia Jones, *Body Art/Performing the Subject* (Minneapolis: University of Minnesota Press, 1998); Jayne Wark, *Radical Gestures: Feminism and Performance Art in North America* (Montreal and Kingston: McGill-Queen's University Press, 2006).

55 Adamson, *Thinking through Craft*, 162.

56 See Kristina Huneault, "Professionalism as Critical Concept and Historical Process for Women and Art in Canada," in Kristina Huneault and Janice Anderson (eds), *Rethinking Professionalism: Women and Art in Canada, 1850-1970* (Montreal and Kingston: McGill-Queen's University Press, 2012), 3–52.

57 Alexandra M. Kokoli, "On Probation: 'Tracey Emin' as Sign," *Wasafiri* 25, no. 1 (2010): 36.

58 Joseph McBrinn, "'Male Trouble': Sewing, Amateurism, and Gender," in Elaine Cheasley Paterson and Susan Surette (eds), *Sloppy Craft: Postdisciplinarity and the Crafts* (London: Bloomsbury, 2015), 30.

59 Lou Cabeen, "Home Work," in Livingstone and Ploof (eds), *The Object of Labour: Art, Cloth, and Cultural Production*, 215–16. Emphasis added.

60 The term "sloppy craft" was first used in 2007 by Art Institute of Chicago artist and educator Anne Wilson to describe the purposeful, "messy" technique adopted by her student, Josh Fraught, in his textile works. Elaine Cheasley Paterson and Susan Surette, "Introduction," in Paterson and Surette (eds), *Sloppy Craft: Postdisciplinarity and the Crafts*, 4.

61 Ibid., 9.

62 Sandra Alfoldy, "Doomed to Failure," in Paterson and Surette (eds), *Sloppy Craft: Postdisciplinarity and the Crafts*, 79.

63 Adamson remarks that "there can be little doubt that Emin is narcissistic, and that the persona she constantly presents to the world is a collage of cherished scars." Adamson, *Thinking through Craft*, 162. Not insignificantly, both drug users/addicts and homosexuals have been identified as "narcissistic" because of their apparent disregard for norms, both societal and sexual. See Lawrence Driscoll, *Reconsidering Drugs: Mapping Victorian and Modern Drug Discourses* (New York: Palgrave, 2000), 57. I do wonder if it is necessary or productive in scholarship on Emin's work to describe her in these terms. Is it narcissistic to discuss women's lived experiences, which for many of us include abortions and alcohol consumption? Are we still not allowed to talk about these things? By extension, are women still not supposed to address these experiences in their art?

64　Cabeen, "Home Work," 211.

65　On the importance of the pose in discourses of decadence, see Dennis Denisoff, "Posing a Threat: Queensberry, Wilde, and the Portrayal of Decadence," in Constable, Denisoff, and Potolsky (eds), *Perennial Decay: On the Aesthetics and Politics of Decadence*, 83–100.

66　Carole S. Vance, "More Danger, More Pleasure: A Decade after the Barnard Sexuality Conference," in Carole S. Vance (ed.), *Pleasure and Danger: Exploring Female Sexuality* (1984; London: Pandora Press, 1992), xvii.

67　Maria Elena Buszek, "Pleasure/Principle," in Maria Elena Buszek and Christophe Kihm (eds), *Ghada Amer: Breathe Into Me* (New York: Gagosian Gallery, 2006), 8.

68　Amer is concerned in some of her work with the veil (the Islamic *hijab*), as a kind of textile that is heavily loaded with both gendered and raced significations. For a discussion on the *hijab* and fashion, see Alexandru Balasescu, "Tehran Chic: Islamic Headscarves, Fashion Designers, and New Geographies of Modernity," *Fashion Theory* 7, no. 1 (March 2003): 34–56.

69　Quoted in Maura Reilly, "Writing the Body: The Art of Ghada Amer," in Maura Reilly (ed.), *Ghada Amer* (New York: Gregory R. Miller & Co., 2010), 15.

70　Thérèse St-Gelais, "The *Others* of Pleasure and Love," in Thérèse St-Gelais (ed.), *Ghada Amer* (Montreal: Musée d'art contemporain de Montréal, 2012), 66.

71　Reilly, "Writing the Body," 21–22.

72　Buszek, "Pleasure/Principle," 3. See also Reilly, "Writing the Body," 23–24.

73　Reilly, "Writing the Body," 18.

74　Ibid., 17.

75　Jackson Pollock is the Abstract Expressionist painter most often invoked in discussions of Amer's work. Reilly, "Writing the Body," 25. According to Reilly, "By 1993, Amer's threaded drips had become even more expressive and a new sense of texture emerged, despite the fact that very little paint was being applied to the canvas, only colored thread" (24). From 1993 to 1995 she had no desire to paint with acrylic at all, stating, "I only wanted to paint with embroidery." Quoted in Reilly, "Writing the Body," 24.

76　The identity, and, indeed, the possibility, of the *flâneuse*, has been provocatively discussed by a number of feminist scholars. See Janet Wolff, "The Invisible *Flâneuse*: Women and the Literature of Modernity," in *Feminine Sentences: Essays on Women and Culture* (Berkeley and Los Angeles: University of California Press, 1990), 34–50. See also Aruna D'Souza and Tom McDonough (eds), *The Invisible* Flâneuse? *Gender, Public Space and Visual Culture in Nineteenth-Century Paris* (Manchester and New York: Manchester University Press, 2006).

77　Carol Duncan, "Virility and Domination in Early Twentieth-Century Vanguard Painting," in *The Aesthetics of Power: Essays in Critical Art History*, 97.

78　Carol Duncan, "The MoMA's Hot Mamas," in *The Aesthetics of Power: Essays in Critical Art History*, 194–5.

79　Melissa Bull, "Preface," in Nelly Arcan (ed.), *Burqa of Skin*, trans. Melissa Bull (Vancouver: Anvil Press, 2014), 14.

80　Ibid., 15.

81　See Echols, *Daring to Be Bad*, 4–5.

82　St-Gelais, "The *Others* of Pleasure and Love," 71–72.

83 Danilo Eccher (ed.), "Ghada Amer," in *Ghada Amer* (Rome: Museo d'Arte Contemporanea Roma, 2007), 92.

84 See Allyson Mitchell (ed.), *Turbo Chicks: Talking Young Feminisms* (Toronto: Sumach Press, 2001).

85 Cvetkovich, *Depression*, 184–5. Emphasis added. On the relationship between excess and waste, see Amanda Boetzkes, *The Ethics of Earth Art* (Minnesota and London: University of Minnesota Press, 2010).

86 Cvetkovich, *Depression*, 173. Emphasis added.

87 Allyson Mitchell "Deep Lez I Statement," in Carla Garnet (ed.), *Allyson Mitchell: Ladies Sasquatch* (Hamilton, ON: The McMaster Museum of Art, 2009), 12.

88 Sarah Quinton, "Threads and Needles," in *When Women Rule the World: Judy Chicago in Thread*, 41.

89 Mitchell, "A Call to Arms," 23. Mitchell curated the exhibition *When Women Rule the World*, which was accompanied by a smaller exhibition, *She Will Always Be Younger than Us*, displaying the works of younger feminist artists who have been influenced by Chicago, including Orly Cogan. Regarding her own art practice, Mitchell has commented: "The objects and environments that I create are about articulating some of the ideas and imaginings of second-wave feminisms that were so foundational to me, while still remaining committed to an inclusive third-wave theory and practice." Mitchell, "Deep Lez I Statement," 12.

90 Bram Dijkstra, *Idols of Perversity: Fantasies of Feminine Evil in Fin-de-Siècle Culture* (Oxford: Oxford University Press, 1986), 240.

91 Cvetkovich, *Depression*, 185.

92 Ann Cvetkovich, "Touching the Monster: Deep Lez in Fun Fur," in Carla Garnet (ed.), *Allyson Mitchell: Ladies Sasquatch*, 29.

93 Josephine Mills, "The Answer is Two Years Spent Baking Vulva-shaped Cookies or, On Understanding Lesbian Representation," in Carla Garnet (ed.), *Allyson Mitchell: Ladies Sasquatch*, 20.

94 Ibid., 24.

95 For more on the idea of queer utopia in Mitchell's work, see Sarah E. K. Smith, "Bringing Queer Theory Into Queer Practice," in *I'm Not Myself At All* (Kingston, ON: Agnes Etherington Art Centre, 2015), 22–31.

96 Quoted in Philippe Jullian, *Dreamers of Decadence: Symbolist Painters of the 1890s*, trans. Robert Baldick (New York: Praeger Publishers, 1971), 43.

97 According to Sarah Quinton: "Allyson Mitchell is hooked on a very specific type of 'collectible'—kitschy mass-produced textile accoutrements such as chenille bedspreads, sunset emblazoned long-pile (shag) rugs, hand-wrought afghan throws and pieces of every-colour-in-the-rainbow fun fur. They are ignored or overlooked, often inexpensively produced and cheap-to-buy forms of culturally loaded flotsam and jetsam that are deeply embedded in lived experience. They have associations of 'unsavoury' aesthetics and faceless mass-consumption." Sarah Quinton (ed.), "Close to You," in *Close to You: Contemporary Textiles, Intimacy and Popular Culture* (Toronto: Textile Museum of Canada, 2007), 20.

98 Cvetkovich, "Touching the Monster," 31.

99 See Elliott, "Housing the Work," 176–91; Bridget Elliott, "Performing the Picture or Painting the Other: Romaine Brooks, Gluck and the Question of Decadence in 1923," in Katy Deepwell (ed.), *Women Artists and Modernism* (Manchester and New York: Manchester University Press, 1998), 70–82; Jasmine Rault, *Staying In: Eileen Gray and the Design of Sapphic Modernity* (Burlington, VT: Ashgate, 2012).

100   "The son of Speranza, who called herself an eagle and thought of herself as Joan of
      Arc, wasted and out of place rocking a cradle, was attracted by heroic women. He said,
      completely seriously, that the women he most admired were Queen Victoria, Lily Langtry, and
      Sarah Bernhardt. All three women were powerful figures in the history of their time. Political,
      sexual, and artistic power, which these three women represent, were rare in females of
      their period." Jane Marcus, *Art and Anger: Reading Like a Woman* (Columbus: Ohio State
      University Press, 1988), 8.

101   For a discussion of *fin-de-siècle* art representing Medusa, see Dijkstra, *Idols of Perversity*, 309.

102   Bernheimer, "Fetishism and Decadence: Salome's Severed Heads," 66.

103   Ibid., 67.

104   Ibid., 76.

105   Ibid., 77. Bernheimer suggests that "Medusa imagery thus becomes, for both Beardsley and
      Wilde, a stimulus to sexual inversion, confusion, and parody, rather than a horrifying symbol
      of emasculation" (80).

106   Carla Garnet (ed.), "Allyson Mitchell: The Ladies Sasquatch, Theory and Practice," in *Allyson
      Mitchell: Ladies Sasquatch*, 17.

107   Hélène Cixous, "The Laugh of the Medusa," in Hilary Robinson (ed.), *Feminism/Art/Theory:
      An Anthology, 1968-2000* (Massachusetts: Blackwell Publishing, 2001), 627–34.

4

"THE DECAYING FABRICS OF LIFE AND DEATH": ROZANNE HAWKSLEY'S TEXTILE ART

In the previous chapters I examined a variety of artworks through the feminist lens of radical decadence. In late-nineteenth-century Europe, moral decay and racial degeneration were regarded as the inevitable aftermath of decadence. As Victoria Kelley reminds us, decay is also part of the life process of textiles.[1] The editors of a book on decadence have discussed the etymological relationship between *decadence* and *decay*, observing: "The general concept of decadence (from the Latin *de* + *cadere*, to fall away or from) centers on decline, decay, and the loss of traditional values."[2] Indeed, the two terms—and ideas— have often been linked through moral discourses related to transgressions of social, or traditional, norms. The Roman Empire was said to have declined after a period of rampant excess, while anxious commentators at the end of the nineteenth century saw parallels between the Roman Empire and the British Empire.[3] In this book it has been my intention to move away from a moralizing, stigmatizing representation of decadence; I have instead offered *radical decadence* as a feminist framework with which to read artworks created out of textiles and porcelain (among other materials) that transgress gendered norms in relation to not only behaviors but also art-historical ideologies.

British artist Rozanne Hawksley's work—which encompasses gloves, installations, masks, and mixed-media works that incorporate velvet, bones, and wood[4]—has previously been described as "decadent" (Plates 13–16). Although Hawksley has been an active artist and teacher for several decades, at present only one monograph has been published on her work. Significantly, in the Preface of that volume, Philip Hughes, director of the Ruthin Craft Centre, comments that "tensions underpin her creativity. They are manifest throughout her work, and in her messages and strategies to engage and draw us in—a combination of opulence, horror, 'decadence' and theatre."[5] Hughes does not elaborate on what he means by "decadence," but it is worth noting that he encloses the word in inverted commas, thereby highlighting the loaded nature of the term.[6]

Design historian Stephen Calloway includes a detail of one of Hawksley's glove works, *And Lead Us Not* (1987–89; Plate 13), as the last image in his book *Baroque Baroque: The Culture of Excess* (1994). In Calloway's book, the glove has been removed from its red satin-lined box and placed instead against a solid gold background where it appears to float. Calloway, like Hughes, does not clarify how Hawksley's work is "excessive" or "decadent," although he asks on the accompanying page: "Who shall say if this baroque of our era is the robust expression of a flourishing culture or the presage, as in other baroque eras, of decadence and decay?"[7] His book, which is a lushly illustrated tome, celebrates "excessive" design through the ages, and yet this passage maintains the historical binary of decadence/decay: decadence as a kind of visual (or behavioral) excess that is followed by an inevitable, deserved decay, implying not only moral degradation but also a decline in artistic value.

Calloway discusses the term "baroque" both as initially pejorative—similar to "decadence"—and as associated with visual excesses. As he explains, "The first objects ever to be called 'baroque' were the bizarre irregular natural pearls so highly prized by collectors in the sixteenth and seventeenth centuries both for their weird beauty and great rarity. The finest became the jealously hoarded treasures of the 'cabinets of curiosities' of princely and noble collectors, wrought by cunning goldsmiths into exquisite jewels in which the magical nacreous form of the pearl became the writhing body of a sea-monster or a demigod."[8] Calloway goes on to consider the origin of the word, which illuminates the paradoxical, threatening albeit pleasurable nature of the baroque: "By a strange etymological quirk, 'baroque,' coined from *barocca*, the word used to describe such pearls, came to have a curious variety of meanings: not merely strong and convoluted, but also extravagant and whimsical, grotesque, and even coarse and vulgar."[9] The term "baroque," then, has at times been a pejorative one, although more recently scholars such as Calloway have appropriated it to consider what others might call "maximalism" or the design-oriented belief that "more is more."[10] These terms, including "baroque," lack the critical, feminist edge that is encoded in *radical decadence*. Significantly, "As a style in architecture, decoration and the decorative arts, the Baroque grew out of the intellectual conceits and *bizarre visual excesses* of the Mannerist phase of the late Renaissance, bringing a new and unparalleled vigour equally to religious and secular art and architecture."[11] The intersections that have occurred between religious visual and material culture and the "baroque" are inevitably woven through with ideas of mortality and life beyond this mortal coil.

Hawksley has described her art as comprising, both literally and symbolically, the "decaying fabrics of life and death."[12] She employs a range of materials, including textiles, wood, sequins, jewels, and bones, and many of her artworks can be described as memento mori, incorporating skull motifs and other allusions to death. One of her preferred mediums is the glove, which has been a constant in her work since the 1950s. Hawksley's literal interest in decay is juxtaposed with her use of such "decadent" materials as velvet and silk. Mary Schoeser has remarked that although Hawksley's "materials range from cloth, jewels and thread to wood, clay and bones, it remains possible to study her approach to the physicality of her work by looking in depth at one medium: the glove. These have been at times the means and, at others, an end in itself."[13] Schoeser goes on to observe that, for Hawksley,

gloves represent those who have used them or made them, as well as the possibility of profound attachment to them and sadness at their loss. Those that are white stand for peace, and for the Royal Marines she loved to watch as a girl. In addition, they are a constant in her work, from the 1950s—when they were required wear for smart young women and, in her first job at Guildford, when she taught the design and making of gloves and belts—to their use in the seminal works of 1987 and 1991 (both sharing in their title the words, *Pale Armistice*) and beyond to the present day. Among her smaller works, those being gloves or composed of gloves are also the most exhibited, giving rise to a body of commentary that allows for an assessment of her place in the continuum of postmodernist and neo-mannerist art.[14]

Hawksley's first *Pale Armistice* (1986–87), a wreath of white gloves, was selected by Pennina Barnett for the groundbreaking *Subversive Stitch* exhibition at Manchester's Cornerhouse Gallery in 1988. A more recent glove work, *Aimez-vous le big Mac?* (Plate 15), is also a memorial glove, this time made of silk chiffon and black fabric woven with gold thread that was being worked into a dress by the deceased, "whose love of nature and the outdoors is signified by the gauntlet lining of blue silk."[15] Like all of her gloves, this work signifies the absent body: both Hawksley's and of those she has lost. There is also an imperfect square of bold pink fabric underneath the glove, which is turned palm-side up, and in the hand is a tarot card (representing a jester-like figure) and a black jester's scepter that is topped with a death's head, or skull. On the tip of the middle finger is a gold thimble. This is a symbolically rich work that speaks not only of the transience of life but also of the sensuous pleasure of materials; with the thimble, Hawksley reminds us that the needle (as sword) can wound, as well as protect and subvert.[16] Compared to the whiteness of *Pale Armistice*, this work's hot pink, gold, and deep black are strikingly decadent color choices.

Hawksley is inspired by, among other things, Victorian mourning customs and costumes.[17] As Beth Fowkes Tobin and Maureen Daly Goggin have observed, "The material culture of death straddles the binaries of life and death, subject and object, production and consumption, private and public, blurring these distinctions, rendering them unstable and in some cases performing dizzying reversals, turning objects into subjects and subjects into objects."[18] Hawksley's use of luxurious fabrics such as velvet and luxurious objects, such as jewelry, have historical precedents in the material culture of death. Arianne Fennetaux discusses how "during the early-modern period, jewelry was among a series of objects that were distributed to mourners and played a role as social markers in the well-orchestrated display of power and hierarchy."[19]

Fennetaux adds: "The aesthetics of mourning jewelry at the end of the seventeenth century borrowed from the traditional repertoire of vanities and included skulls, bones, and coffins as visual signals meant to provoke reflection on the common fate of human death. Mourning rings that were distributed to mourners at funerals with their iconography of skulls, crossed bones, or grim skeletons acted as a sobering reminder of human frailty. The death of others was a moment for the living to reflect on their coming death."[20] Hawksley portrays a half-skeleton, half-woman figure on the back of her mask *One has to be so careful these days* (Figure 4.1). The woman, naked and heavily made up, appears blissfully unaware of her deathly half. Likewise, in *A Vanitas Portrait of a Lady Believed to be Clara Peeters* (Figure 4.2), a young woman, concerned with earthly matters, is surrounded by symbols of transience, such as a bubble and flowers. Perhaps the most

Figure 4.1 Rozanne Hawksley, *One has to be so careful these days*, 2004. Face mask. Courtesy of artist and Philip Hughes of Ruthin Craft Centre.

Figure 4.2 Clara Peeters (1594–1659), *A Vanitas Portrait of a Lady Believed to be Clara Peeters/* Private Collection/Photo ©Bonhams, London UK/Bridgeman Images.

conspicuous symbol of *vanitas* is the jewelry that adorns the female subject's head, neck, wrists, and table.

While many of her works are concerned with death, and with grief, I want to suggest that Hawksley's oeuvre is not "merely" a modernized version of *Vanitas* paintings or memento mori. Furthermore, although Schoeser suggests that we can read Hawksley's artworks as a reminder to *not* engage in "trivial pleasures," I propose that we instead read in these art objects a dialogue between decadence and decay, pleasure and pain.[21] An alternate reading of Hawksley's oeuvre opens space for the rejection of the belief that (moral) decay *must* follow decadence, or that pain *must* follow pleasure as a form of moral punishment; rather, it is possible to see in Hawksley's work a sensuous engagement with lives that have been lived fully, "excessively" even. This kind of life invariably entails experiencing *both* pleasure and pain. Even as Hawksley's artworks remind us of death, they are, after all, pleasurable to look at, at least in part because of the materials she chooses to work with.[22]

As noted in Chapter 1, drug use was identified as decadent at the *fin de siècle*, and more recent scholars, such as Timothy Hickman, have noted that the drug user or addict is still expected to have a certain "look": "wasted, decadent, desperate."[23] I return to drug use briefly in this final chapter in order to argue that it is only one form of radical decadence that entails both pleasure and pain. In *Confessions of an English Opium Eater* (1821), Thomas de Quincey, one of the most famous addicts of English literature, speaks eloquently of the pleasure and pain that is (sometimes) part of addiction.[24] Hawksley, unlike Orly Cogan (Plate 2), is not concerned with drug use in her work, yet her art illuminates the fact that pain and pleasure are not limited to drug users and addicts. Both artists, however, have produced works that incorporate mirrors: Hawksley's *Black Mirror* and *White Mirror*, both from 2004, anticipate Cogan's *Mirror, Mirror* (Plate 3), which depicts a young woman preparing to snort cocaine off the eponymous object.[25] We will recall from Chapter 2 that Canadian artist Shary Boyle's sculpture *To Colonize the Moon* (Plate 6) also incorporates a mirror in a scene that depicts a decapitated Medusa figure and a Narcissus-like figure inspired by a seventeenth-century bronze sculpture. Another work by Hawksley, *Goe and catche a falling starre*, a mask from 2003, is studded with mirrors, reminding us of the importance of both masks and mirrors in late-nineteenth-century discourses of decadence.[26] There is also a small circular mirror on Hawksley's *One has to be so careful these days* (Figure 4.1).

Is it merely coincidence that these three artists, all born in different countries, have produced works that employ mirrors for various purposes? Certainly, in this book, I have brought together the work of Boyle, Cogan, and Hawksley, as well as that of Nava Lubelski, Mickalene Thomas, and Tracey Emin, among others, because I see in their art echoes, as well as rejections, of *fin de siècle* decadent objects, decadent acts, and decadent ideas. The mirror, of course, has been used throughout the history of art to signify female vanity. Schoeser alludes to this history when she writes that Hawksley's "much later mirrors, embellished with jewels, lace, sequins and feathers, have an innocence as if filtered through the eyes and emotions of this young woman—a beauty derived from the tenderness with which each element is incorporated—and yet a sternness that rebukes the folly of vanity, and perhaps of decisions quickly made and regretted."[27] Must one regret so-called follies? In Cogan's work, the mirror does not signify female vanity, but rather drug use, perhaps in the name of pleasure. As I noted in a previous chapter, the idea of guilty pleasures has generally been gendered as a feminine affect. Must certain kinds of pleasure for women always be guilty and therefore regretted?

Like the "guilty pleasure," the act of "making a spectacle of oneself," according to Mary Russo, is a "specifically feminine danger."[28] One characteristic of radical decadence that I hope to have drawn out in the previous chapters is a willingness to take risks despite knowledge of the (potential) consequences: creating art that (ostensibly) makes a "spectacle" of the artist, employing crafty or "kitschy" materials, representing alcohol and drug use, transgressing or refusing expected "feminine" roles, producing art that alludes to abortion, openly experiencing same-sex desire, coming out as a drug user or addict.[29] All of these acts entail risk. I will once more cite Mary Russo, who has written that to live excessively (as a woman) is fundamentally to live riskily. As Russo remarks, "I would point out that the grotesque in each case is only recognizable in relation to a norm and that exceeding the norm involves serious risk."[30] All of the artists discussed in *Radical Decadence* have taken, and continue to take, risks. Hawksley has stated that "all work is a risk."[31] Her work is decadent not only because she employs velvet and silk, although this choice of materials speaks to histories of luxury, sumptuary laws, pleasure, and, surely, financial strain and aspirational living that has consequences of its own.[32] John Potvin has discussed the significance of specific materials, observing that

> fabrics like velvet (a textile once exclusive to the aristocracy given the time and cost associated with it), also disclose the possibility of perversion or the subversion of the dominant bourgeois ethos. The formidable fictional, if somewhat autobiographical, much celebrated and maligned decadent novel *A Rebours* (*Against Nature*) (1884) by J.K. Huysmans narrates the exquisite and idiosyncratic life of Jean Des Esseintes. . . . Renouncing his sumptuary proclivities and decadent bachelor days in Paris, the novel's protagonist removes himself to the countryside where in contemplative solace, consoles himself with a world of his own divination.[33]

Potvin continues: "It was not simply that he used velvet, but that it was white, marking out a unique and idiosyncratic individuation through fabric, at once material/visual, aesthetic/ascetic, public/private. Artifice was his mantra and lifestyle. Like Miss O'Hara's use of green velvet," in *Gone With the Wind*, "Des Esseintes's use of the fabric, only made accessible to and popular by the middle class in the early nineteenth century, is marked by a twist of decadence—making it his own, claiming an individual relationship to body, space and fabric."[34] As I have already noted, Hawksley's oeuvre is radically decadent not only because she employs velvet, among other materials, but also in the (perhaps more important) sense that as a woman artist she has produced risky artworks that speak to loss, grief, and death, employing mirrors, skulls, and jewels that are not, to my mind, the moralizing signifiers of historical *Vanitas* paintings, but rather glimmers of pleasure in the dark.

In *Libera me, domine, de morte aeterna* (*Deliver me, oh Lord, from eternal death*) (Plate 14), according to Mary Schoeser, the jewelled skull represents life on earth, and the three pearls symbolize the Trinity.[35] Jeremy Biles has discussed British artist Damien Hirst's jewelled skull, *For the Love of God* (2007), arguing that it articulates the "ambivalence of excess." Biles quotes Hirst about his reasons for covering a skull with diamonds: "I just want to celebrate life by saying to hell with death. What better way of saying that than by taking the ultimate symbol of death and covering it in the ultimate symbol of luxury, desire and decadence?"[36] All is transience, yes, but Hawksley's work encourages us, if we let it, to live to the hilt. According to Audrey Walker, in correspondence with Schoeser in 2008, "Courage" and "No compromises" are "the marks of her work. Over the years she has exploded any pre-conceived notions of what a 'textile work' can be, in either form or subject matter. The work can be sumptuous or spare, tiny or room-size, and layered with symbolic references. It exists in that perilous area where categorisation is impossible and, as such, it continues to challenge us all."[37] Like the other artists discussed in this book, Hawksley's work is "risky" in part *because* it employs textiles and, as Walker notes, because she challenges not only ideas about what a textile artwork can be, but also ideas about what a woman artist should or should not do.

In a book about baroque visual rhetoric, Vernon Hyde Minor notes Freud's observation that artists in ancient Egypt tended to "form images of the dead in durable materials."[38] What do we make of Hawksley's work, then, which is so tied up with death? Her artworks are made with, if not necessarily fragile materials (even durable materials are, after all, ephemeral, transient), materials that are soft, flexible, pleasurable to the touch (and the eye), velvety, silky. They are the opposite of those durable materials of ancient Egypt. The transience of even the most durable materials functions as memento mori—remember that you shall die: from dust to dust. Hawksley's materials are not the hard materials that are meant to (unsuccessfully) deny death, but rather the materials of pleasure and luxury, opulence and desire. Janis Jefferies observes: "The softness and ultimate fragility of cloth are linked to organic bodily matter and the vulnerability of humans, whose every relationship is transient, subject to the degenerative process of decay and death."[39] Rather than denying death, Hawksley's artworks acknowledge death as inevitable, but life is, if we are very lucky, full of pleasure, some of it tactile, sensual, even sexual; some of it visual, visible, and sometimes illusionary—but all of it fleeting. Her works are not moralizing; nor do they cast judgment upon us for wanting to experience pleasure in our lifetime. Rather, they offer us, the beholders of these works, pleasures that may be transient, but that remain in photographs, books, museums, collections, and our own mind palaces, until those too, crumble. As Sue Rowley has remarked: "Craftwork teaches us to die, and by doing so teaches us to live."[40]

There is no one way to produce "radically decadent" art, just as there is no one way to "read" radical decadence from a work as a (feminist) scholar. What I have tried to do in this book is to illuminate that living "excessively" as a woman, whether one identifies as a feminist or not, is to take risks despite knowledge of the (potential) consequences. I have moved away from the moralizing, pathologizing perception of decadence that was popular at the *fin de siècle*,[41] arguing instead that excess and decadence, for women, can be liberating *because* both are inherently founded on a rejection, or refusal, of ideal femininity that is still, to my horror, associated (by some) with silence.[42]

As I was completing this book, I finally got around to reading Rebecca Solnit's *Men Explain Things to Me*. In that essay, and the accompanying essays, Solnit shows incontrovertibly that the way that (some) men explain things to (some) women cannot be separated from ongoing, systemic violence against women.[43] In fact, I began writing this conclusion the day after the twenty-sixth anniversary of a man going into a Montreal college and shooting fourteen women, because, apparently, he was angry about "feminism." I had not intended to conclude *Radical Decadence* with violence, but that moment in history, in Montreal where I live and work, continues to haunt us because we (or at least some of us) know that women are still at risk.[44] According to Russo, "The risk of such leaps and flights lies in the danger of the fatal fall. The impasse of this modernist symbolization for the entity marked 'Woman' is that there is only one way out: death, whatever its representation—hysterical breakdown, unconsciousness, loss of visibility, or more literally loss of life."[45] Russo's statement recalls the fate of the nineteenth-century femme fatale,[46] as well as the female drug user of twentieth-century films.[47] Her observation also resonates when we consider what Rebecca Solnit calls "the longest war," that is, the war on women that encompasses everything from insidious forms of silencing to murder.[48]

In *Radical Decadence* I have discussed a range of artworks, all of them brightly colored—in stark contrast to Aubrey Beardsley's decadent black-and-white drawings for *Salomé*—which represent or refer to acts that result in pleasure, including drug use, drinking, eating, self-fashioning through clothes and cosmetics, and sex. Cogan's title *Bittersweet Obsession* reminds us, if we ever had a chance to forget (which I doubt), that there is sometimes, though certainly not always, a darker side to pleasure. This is not to pathologize pleasure, but rather to acknowledge the realities that can go hand in hand with those behaviors that offer pleasure: hangovers, STIs, debt. These are some of the realities, the possible consequences, of those acts that I have discussed in *Radical Decadence*. But certain groups and individuals have *used* those *possible* consequences to moralize and thus try to control women who engage in those behaviors, identifying them as "excessive."

To live excessively, as a woman, is to take risks. It is to experience both pleasure and pain. It is to refuse to be silenced, whether in art or life, to be turned into a good girl who toes the line. It has not been my intention in this book to simplistically promote any of the "risky" behaviors that radically decadent artists have dealt with. Lauren Berlant has argued in *Cruel Optimism* that various coping methods, such as (excessive) food consumption, are ultimately counterproductive.[49] As she observes:

> A relation of cruel optimism exists when something you desire is actually an obstacle to your flourishing. It might involve food, or a kind of love; it might be a fantasy of the good life, or a political project. It might rest on something simpler, too, like a new habit that promises to induce in you an improved way of being. These kinds of optimistic relations are not inherently cruel. They become cruel only when the object that draws your attachment actively impedes the aim that brought you to it initially.[50]

The artists discussed in *Radical Decadence* have pushed against the art/craft hierarchy, while also pushing against sexist, racist, and homophobic ideologies, in artworks that often, though not always, represent or allude to some of those "habits" to which Berlant refers. Some of the artists explicitly engage with behaviors often deemed "excessive," while others have been more concerned with exceeding gendered, sexed, and raced norms related to women and women artists. All of them, I suggest, are radically decadent not only because of their choice of materials, but also because they have taken risks in both their artworks and their lives, even when it means being the unwelcome guest at the proverbial dinner party (Plate 1 and Figure 4.3).

Figure 4.3 Julie Heffernan, *Self-Portrait as Unwelcome Guest*, 1997. Oil on canvas, 96.52 × 152.4 cm. Pennsylvania Academy of the Fine Arts, Philadelphia. Art by Women Collection, Gift of Linda Lee Alter. Copyright: 1997 Julie Heffernan.

Notes

1 "The decay that time and use visit upon textile objects is insistent and inexorable, while resistance to it in the work of cleanliness and maintenance is both heroic and ultimately futile, patterned by repetitions and cyclical procedures, and inevitably, at the period in which I am interested, associated with class status and difference, and with strictly gendered domestic labor." Victoria Kelley, "The Interpretation of Surface: Boundaries, Systems and their Transgression in Clothing and Domestic Textiles, *c.*1880-1939," *Textile: The Journal of Cloth & Culture* 7, no. 2 (July 2009): 220–21. See also Julia Skelly, "Object Lessons: The Social Life of Temperance Banners," *Textile: The Journal of Cloth and Culture* 14, no. 3 (2016): 268–93.

2 Constable, Potolsky, and Denisoff, "Introduction," 2.

3 See Lynda Nead, *Victorian Babylon: People, Streets, and Images in Nineteenth-Century London* (New Haven and London: Yale University Press, 2000).

4 For instance, *From a Jack to a King—Greed* (1998), which was included in the exhibition *On the Edge*, curated by Julia Caprara. The exhibition questioned "the boundaries of embroidery." Mary Schoeser, *Rozanne Hawksley* (North Wales and Farnham, UK/Burlington, VT: Ruthin Craft Centre and Lund Humphries, 2009), 67. The mixed-media work depicts a skeletal nude male figure seated atop a tree stump inside a purple velvet-lined wardrobe with gold accents and a purple curtain behind him. He wears a crown, holds a gold scepter with an unfurling banner made out of metal, and his left foot is placed on top of a globe. His face is sunken and contorted into what could be interpreted as either a laugh or a scream. The work is both beautiful and disturbing.

5 Philip Hughes, "Preface," in Mary Schoeser (ed.), *Rozanne Hawksley* (North Wales and Farnham, UK/Burlington, VT: Ruthin Craft Centre and Lund Humphries, 2009), 9.

6 For more on this, see Richard Gilman, *Decadence: The Strange Life of an Epithet* (New York: Farrar, Straus, and Giroux, 1975).

7 Stephen Calloway, *Baroque Baroque: The Culture of Excess* (London: Phaidon Press, 1994), 232.

8 Ibid., 7.

9 Ibid.

10 Mary Schoeser, *More is More: An Antidote to Minimalism* (London: Conran Octopus, 2001).

11 Calloway, *Baroque Baroque*, 7. Emphasis added.

12 Quoted in Schoeser, *Rozanne Hawksley*, 102.

13 Ibid., 171.

14 Ibid.

15 Ibid., 181.

16 Sue Carter, "Using the Needle as a Sword: Needlework as Epideictic Rhetoric in the Woman's Christian Temperance Union," in Patricia Bizzell (ed.), *Rhetorical Agendas: Political, Ethical, Spiritual* (Mahwah, NJ, and London: Lawrence Erlbaum Publishers, 2006), 325–35.

17 Schoeser, *Rozanne Hawksley*, 164.

18 Beth Fowkes Tobin and Maureen Daly Goggin, "Connecting Women and Death: An Introduction," in Goggin and Tobin (eds), *Women and the Material Culture of Death*, 2.

19 Arianne Fennetaux, "Fashioning Death/Gendering Sentiment: Mourning Jewelry in Britain in the Eighteenth Century," in Goggin and Tobin (eds), *Women and the Material Culture of Death*, 27.

20 Ibid., 33.

21 Schoeser, *Rozanne Hawksley*, 178.

22 For more on the material culture of death, see Marcia Pointon, "Materializing Mourning: Hair, Jewellery and the Body," in Marius Kwint, Christopher Breward and Jeremy Aynsley (eds), *Material Memories: Design and Evocation* (Oxford and New York: Berg, 1999), 39–57. Charles Bernheimer has remarked: "Lacan comments that 'the point of the gaze always participates in the ambiguity of the jewel.' That ambiguity, as I understand it, resides in the way the jewel's beauty, rather than reinforcing narcissism as one might expect of an ornament, actually reflects the subject's dissolution in the field of the other. This analysis illuminates a crucial function of jewels and gems in decadent literature: they are not merely decorative objects but, more significantly, emblems of the subject's attraction to death." Bernheimer's observation furthers our interpretation of Hawksley's work as "decadent." Charles Bernheimer, *Decadent Subjects: The Idea of Decadence in Art, Literature, Philosophy, and Culture of the* Fin de Siècle *in Europe*, eds. T. Jefferson Kline and Naomi Schor (Baltimore and London: Johns Hopkins University Press, 2002), 108–09.

23 Timothy A. Hickman, "Heroin Chic: The Visual Culture of Narcotic Addiction," *Third Text* 16, no. 2 (2002): 119.

24 See also Barry Milligan, *Pleasures and Pains: Opium and the Orient in Nineteenth-Century British Culture* (Charlottesville and London: University Press of Virginia, 1995).

25 According to Schoeser, "Reinventing discarded objects, giving them a new artistic life, is a lynchpin" of Hawksley's "approach to materials. *Black Mirror* (2004) is also embellished with bones, as is its companion, *White Mirror*. The mirrors allude to Jean Cocteau's surrealistic film, *Orphée*, which was released in 1950 and includes the storyline that death comes and goes through a mirror." Schoeser, *Rozanne Hawksley*, 56.

26 See, especially, Max Beerbohm, "A Defence of Cosmetics"; Arthur Symons's "Maquillage"; and Oscar Wilde, "The Decay of Lying: An Observation." All of these texts are included in Karl Beckson (ed.), *Aesthetes and Decadents of the 1890s: An Anthology of British Poetry and Prose* (Chicago: Academy Chicago Publishers, 1981).

27 Schoeser, *Rozanne Hawksley*, 57.

28 Mary Russo, *The Female Grotesque: Risk, Excess and Modernity* (New York and London: Routledge, 1994), 53.

29 "In the case of drug addicts, we can pretty much adopt the notion of [the] closet without worrying too much: drug addicts *are* (perhaps) the last minority to be forced, legally, morally, and culturally, into the closet, without really having the option of coming out." Maurizio Viano, "An Intoxicated Screen: Reflections on Film and Drugs," in Janet Farrell Brodie and Marc Redfield (eds), *High Anxieties: Cultural Studies in Addiction* (Berkeley: University of California Press, 2002), 150.

30 Russo, *The Female Grotesque*, 10.

31 Quoted in Schoeser, *Rozanne Hawksley*, 181.

32 In his discussion of anti-drug rhetoric, Kane Race observes: "At about this time, a word entered Australian political discourse with such force, and with such an apparent monopoly on its signification, that I found myself wondering whether I had ever understood the real sense of the term. The election, by all accounts, hinged on the voting patterns of the new 'aspirational' class. *Aspiration* was taken to denote mobility—both 'upward' and 'outward,' economic and geographic. A mortgage-holding, double-income, upwardly mobile, lower-middle class was constructed, resident in the outskirts of major cities." Kane Race, *Pleasure Consuming Medicine: The Queer Politics of Drugs* (Durham, NC, and London: Duke University Press, 2009), 81.

33 John Potvin, "The Velvet Masquerade: Fashion, Interior Design and the Furnished Body," in Myzelev and Potvin (eds), *Fashion, Interior Design and the Contours of Modern Identity*, 5.

34 Ibid., 6.

35 Schoeser, *Rozanne Hawksley*, 178.

36 Quoted in Jeremy Biles, "For the Love of God: Excess, Ambivalence, and Damien Hirst's Diamond Skull," in Skelly (ed.), *The Uses of Excess in Visual and Material Culture, 1600-2010*, 225.

37 Schoeser, *Rozanne Hawksley*, 164.

38 Vernon Hyde Minor, *Baroque Visual Rhetoric* (Toronto: University of Toronto Press, 2016), 56.

39 Janis Jefferies, "Laboured Cloth: Translations of Hybridity in Contemporary Art," in Livingstone and Ploof (eds), *The Object of Labour: Art, Cloth, and Cultural Production*, 284.

40 Sue Rowley, "Craft, Creativity and Critical Practice," in Sue Rowley (ed.), *Reinventing Textiles*, vol. 1: Tradition & Innovation (Winchester, UK: Telos, 1999), 15.

41 Max Nordau, *Degeneration* (1892; Lincoln and London: University of Nebraska Press, 2006).

42 As I noted in the Introduction, late-nineteenth-century "decadence . . . can often be defined in terms of refusals," which, according to Edward Lucie-Smith, "calls attention to the generally negative aspects of the Symbolist emotional climate. Symbolism was a way of saying 'no' to a number of things which were contemporary with itself." Edward Lucie-Smith, *Symbolist Art* (London: Thames and Hudson, 1993), 54.

43 Rebecca Solnit, *Men Explain Things to Me* (Chicago: Haymarket Books, 2014).

44 On women who are particularly vulnerable to violence, see Claudette Lauzon, "What the Body Remembers: Rebecca Belmore's Memorial to Missing Women," in Olivier Asselin, Johanne Lamoureux, and Christine Ross (eds), *Precarious Visualities: New Perspectives on Identification in Contemporary Art and Visual Culture* (Montreal and Kingston: McGill-Queen's University Press, 2008), 155–79.

45 Russo, *The Female Grotesque*, 44–45.

46 See, for example, George Ross Ridge, "The 'Femme Fatale' in French Decadence," *The French Review* 34, no. 4 (February 1961): 352–60. According to Ridge, beginning with a reference to poet Charles Baudelaire, in late-nineteenth-century decadent literature (by men),

"Man is a weak decadent consumed by modern woman, a vampire or *femme fatale*" (352). Because the late nineteenth century was a period of increased advocacy for women's rights, as well as the historical moment of the New Woman, anxieties about gender resulted in literary and visual representations of the femme fatale, who was often killed off for her trouble. Significantly, as Elizabeth K. Menon has discussed, the femme fatale also became "a symbol for the addictive substance that at first evoked aversion, but later caused sensual pleasure: the first cigarette caused choking; a first drink of absinthe tasted bitter." Menon, "Decadent Addictions: Tobacco, Alcohol, Popular Imagery, and Café Culture in France," 104. For more on the New Woman, see Linda Dowling, "The Decadent and the New Woman in the 1890's," *Nineteenth-Century Fiction* 33, no. 4 (March 1979): 434–53, and Mary Louise Roberts, *Disruptive Acts: The New Woman in Fin-de-Siècle France* (Chicago: University of Chicago Press, 2002).

47 Susan C. Boyd, *Hooked: Drug War Films in Britain, Canada, and the United States* (Toronto: University of Toronto Press, 2008), 148.

48 Rebecca Solnit, "The Longest War," in *Men Explain Things to Me* (Chicago: Haymarket Books, 2014), 19–38.

49 On coping, in the context of depression, see Christine Ross, *The Aesthetics of Disengagement: Contemporary Art and Depression* (Minneapolis and London: University of Minnesota Press, 2006).

50 Lauren Berlant, *Cruel Optimism* (Durham, NC, and London: Duke University Press, 2011), 1. Berlant's observations on excess, specifically fatness, are significant for what she illuminates regarding race, among other things: "To the extent that emaciation in the United States remains coded as white and weight excess coded as black, the so-called crisis of obesity continues to juggle the symbolic burden of class signified through the elision of whiteness from the racial marking of poverty; these markings, at minimum, not only shape particular aversions to the people of excess (already negated as both too much and too little for ordinary social membership) but also the topic of excess as a general issue of public health. One way around this racialization of obesity has been the obfuscation of distinctions among the merely overweight, the obese, and the morbidly obese in the crisis rhetoric of care. Still, the phrase *morbidly obese* seems so frequently to raise the African American specter in ways that reinforce the image of African Americans as a population already saturated by death and available for mourning, compelled by appetites rather than by strategies of sovereign agency toward class mobility. People of color generally stand in, in the discourse of obesity, for the entire culture of U.S. nonelites. The word *culture* here is no accident; as food practices seem more cultural, obesity can seem less related to the conditions of labor, schooling, and zoning that construct the endemic environment of the 'epidemic's' emergence." Berlant, *Cruel Optimism*, 112–13.

BIBLIOGRAPHY

Adamson, Glenn (ed.). *The Craft Reader* (Oxford and New York: Berg, 2010).

Adamson, Glenn. *The Invention of Craft* (London: Bloomsbury, 2013).

Adamson, Glenn. *Thinking Through Craft* (Oxford and New York: Berg, 2007).

Ahmed, Sara. "Killing Joy: Feminism and the History of Happiness," *Signs: Journal of Women in Culture and Society* 35, no. 3 (2010): 571–94.

Alfoldy, Sandra. *The Allied Arts: Architecture and Craft in Postwar Canada* (Montreal and Kingston: McGill-Queen's University Press, 2012).

Alfoldy, Sandra. "Doomed to Failure," in Elaine Cheasley Paterson and Susan Surette (eds), *Sloppy Craft: Postdisciplinarity and the Crafts* (London: Bloomsbury, 2015), 79–92.

Alfoldy, Sandra. "Introduction," in Sandra Alfoldy (ed.), *NeoCraft: Modernity and the Crafts* (Nova Scotia, Halifax: The Press of the Nova Scotia College of Art and Design, 2007), xiv–xxii.

Alpers, Svetlana. "Art History and Its Exclusions: The Example of Dutch Art," in Norma Broude and Mary D. Garrard (eds), *Feminism and Art History: Questioning the Litany* (New York: Harper & Row, 1982), 183–99.

Anderson, Tammy L. "Dimensions of Women's Power in the Illicit Drug Economy," *Theoretical Criminology* 9, no. 4 (2005): 371–400.

Archer-Straw, Petrine. *Negrophilia: Avant-Garde Paris and Black Culture in the 1920s* (New York: Thames & Hudson, 2000).

Auther, Elissa. *String, Felt, Thread: The Hierarchy of Art and Craft in American Art* (Minneapolis and London: University of Minnesota Press, 2010).

Balasescu, Alexandru. "Tehran Chic: Islamic Headscarfs, Fashion Designers, and New Geographies of Modernity," *Fashion Theory* 7, no. 1 (March 2003): 34–56.

Beckett, Jane. "Engendering the Spaces of Modernity: The Women's Exhibition, Amsterdam 1913," in Bridget Elliott and Janice Helland (eds), *Women Artists and the Decorative Arts, 1880-1935: The Gender of Ornament* (Aldershot, UK and Burlington, VT: Ashgate, 2002), 155–75.

Beckson, Karl (ed.). *Aesthetes and Decadents of the 1890's: An Anthology of British Poetry and Prose* (Chicago: Academy Chicago Publishers, 1981).

Beerbohm, Max. "A Defence of Cosmetics," in Karl Beckson (ed.), *Aesthetes and Decadents of the 1890's* (Chicago: Academy Chicago Publishers, 1993), 47–63.

Berlant, Lauren. *Cruel Optimism* (Durham, NC, and London: Duke University Press, 2011).

Bernheimer, Charles. *Decadent Subjects: The Idea of Decadence in Art, Literature, Philosophy, and Culture of the* Fin de Siècle *in Europe*, eds. T. Jefferson Kline and Naomi Schor (Baltimore and London: Johns Hopkins University Press, 2002).

Bernheimer, Charles. "Fetishism and Decadence: Salome's Severed Heads," in Emily Apter and William Pketz (eds), *Fetishism as Cultural Discourse* (Ithaca and London: Cornell University Press, 1993), 62–83.

Betterton, Rosemary. "Body Horror?: Food (and Sex and Death) in Women's Art," in *An Intimate Distance: Women, Artists and the Body* (New York and London: Routledge, 1996), 130–60.

Betterton. Rosemary. "'A Perfect Woman': The Political Body of Suffrage," in *An Intimate Distance: Women, Artists and the Body* (New York and London: Routledge, 1996), 46–78.

Biles, Jeremy. "For the Love of God: Excess, Ambivalence, and Damien Hirst's Diamond Skull," in Julia Skelly (ed.), *The Uses of Excess in Visual and Material Culture, 1600-2010* (Farnham: Ashgate, 2014), 225–47.

Bishop, Claire. *Artificial Hells: Participatory Art and the Politics of Spectatorship* (London and New York: Verso, 2012).

Bjerg, Ole. "Drug Addiction and Capitalism: Too Close to the Body," *Body & Society* 14, no. 2 (June 2008): 1–22.

Boetzkes, Amanda. *The Ethics of Earth Art* (Minnesota and London: University of Minnesota Press, 2010).

Bourriaud, Nicolas. *Relational Aesthetics* (Paris: Le Presses due reel, 1998; translated 2002).

Boyd, Susan C. *From Witches to Crack Moms: Women, Drug Law, and Policy* (Durham, NC: Carolina Academic Press, 2004).

Boyd, Susan C. *Hooked: Drug War Films in Britain, Canada, and the United States* (Toronto: University of Toronto Press, 2008).

Boyle, Shary. *Otherworld Uprising* (Montreal: Conundrum Press, 2008).

Brevik-Zender, Heidi. "Decadent Decors and Torturous Textiles: Fatal Fashions and Interior Design in the Fin-de-Siècle Novels of Rachilde," in John Potvin and Alla Myzelev (eds), *Fashion, Interior Design and the Contours of Modern Identity* (Farnham and Burlington, VT: Ashgate, 2010), 105–23.

Brock, Dan W. "Can Pleasure Be Bad for You?," *The Hastings Center Report* 13, no. 4 (August 1983): 30–34.

Broude, Norma. "Miriam Schapiro and 'Femmage': Reflections on the Conflict Between Decoration and Abstraction in Twentieth-Century Art," in Norma Broude and Mary D. Garrard (eds), *Feminism and Art History: Questioning the Litany* (New York: Harper & Row, 1982), 315–29.

Brown, Neal. *Tracey Emin* (London: Tate Publishing, 2006).

Bruno, Giuliana. *Surface: Matters of Aesthetics, Materiality, and Media* (Chicago: University of Chicago Press, 2014).

Buckley, Cheryl. "Ceramics," in Fiona Carson and Claire Pajaczkowska (eds), *Feminist Visual Culture* (New York and London: Routledge, 2001), 171–87.

Bull, Melissa. "Preface," in Nelly Arcan (ed.), *Burqa of Skin*, trans. Melissa Bull (Vancouver: Anvil Press, 2014), 9–26.

Buszek, Maria Elena. "Introduction: The Ordinary Made Extra/Ordinary," in Maria Elena Buszek (ed.), *Extra/Ordinary: Craft and Contemporary Art* (Durham, NC and London: Duke University Press, 2011), 1–19.

Buszek, Maria Elena. "Pleasure/Principle," in Maria Elena Buszek and Christophe Kihm (eds), *Ghada Amer: Breathe Into Me* (New York: Gagosian Gallery, 2006), 3–12.

Cabeen, Lou. "Home Work," in Joan Livingstone and John Ploof (eds), *The Object of Labour: Art, Cloth, and Cultural Production* (Chicago: School of the Art Institute of Chicago Press, 2007), 197–218.

Callen, Anthea. *Women in the Arts and Crafts Movement, 1870-1914* (London: Astragal Books, 1980).

Calloway, Stephen. *Baroque Baroque: The Culture of Excess* (London: Phaidon Press, 1994).

Campbell, Nerida (ed.). "Femme Fatale: The Female Criminal," in *Femme Fatale: The Female Criminal* (Sydney: Historic Houses Trust of New South Wales, 2008), 4–15.

Carter, Sue. "Using the Needle as a Sword: Needlework as Epideictic Rhetoric in the Woman's Christian Temperance Union," in Patricia Bizzell (ed.), *Rhetorical Agendas: Political, Ethical, Spiritual* (Mahwah, NJ and London: Lawrence Erlbaum Publishers, 2006), 325–35.

Chari, Hema. "Imperial Dependence, Addiction, and the Decadent Body," in Liz Constable, Dennis Denisoff and Matthew Potolsky (eds), *Perennial Decay: On the Aesthetics and Politics of Decadence* (Philadelphia: University of Pennsylvania, 1999), 215–32.

Chedgzoy, Kate. "Frida Kahlo's 'Grotesque' Bodies," in P. Florence and D. Reynolds (eds), *Feminist Subjects, Multi-Media: Cultural Methodologies* (Manchester: Manchester University Press, 1995), 39–53.

Cheng, Anne Anlin. *Second Skin: Josephine Baker and the Modern Surface* (Oxford and New York: Oxford University Press, 2011).

Cherry, Deborah. "On the Move: *My Bed*, 1998-1999," in Mandy Merck and Chris Townsend (eds), *The Art of Tracey Emin* (London: Thames & Hudson, 2002), 134–54.

Cixous, Hélène. "The Laugh of the Medusa," in Hilary Robinson (ed.), *Feminism/Art/Theory: An Anthology, 1968-2000* (Massachusetts: Blackwell Publishing, 2001), 627–34.

Collins, Patricia Hill. *Black Feminist Thought: Knowledge, Consciousness, and the Politics of Empowerment* (New York: Routledge, 1990).

Constable, Liz, Matthew Potolsky, and Dennis Denisoff. "Introduction," in Liz Constable, Dennis Denisoff, and Matthew Potolsky (eds), *Perennial Decay: On the Aesthetics and Politics of Decadence* (Philadelphia: University of Pennsylvania Press, 1999), 1–32.

Cook, Sharon Anne. *Canadian Women, Smoking, and Visual Culture, 1880-2000* (Montreal and Kingston: McGill-Queen's University Press, 2012).

Creed, Barbara. *The Monstrous-Feminine: Film, Feminism, Psychoanalysis* (New York and London: Routledge, 1993).

Cvetkovich, Ann. *Depression: A Public Feeling* (Durham, NC and London: Duke University Press, 2012).

Cvetkovich, Ann. "Touching the Monster: Deep Lez in Fun Fur," in Carla Garnet (ed.), *Allyson Mitchell: Ladies Sasquatch* (Hamilton, ON: The McMaster Museum of Art, 2009), 26–31.

Denisoff, Dennis. "Posing a Threat: Queensberry, Wilde, and the Portrayal of Decadence," in Liz Constable, Dennis Denisoff, and Matthew Potolsky (eds), *Perennial Decay: On the Aesthetics and Politics of Decadence* (Philadelphia, PA: University of Pennsylvania, 1999), 83–100.

Déry, Louise (ed.). "The Redemption of the Senses," in *Shary Boyle: Flesh and Blood* (Montreal: Galerie l'UQAM, 2010), 103–26.

Dickson, Rachel (ed.). "Introduction," in *Judy Chicago and Louise Bourgeois, Helen Chadwick, Tracey Emin* (London: Lund Humphries, 2012), 8–13.

Dijkstra, Bram. *Idols of Perversity: Fantasies of Feminine Evil in Fin-de-Siècle Culture* (Oxford: Oxford University Press, 1986).

Doane, Mary Ann. *Femmes Fatales: Feminism, Film Theory, Psychoanalysis* (New York and London: Routledge, 1991).

Douglas, Mary Ann. *Purity and Danger: An Analysis of Concepts of Pollution and Taboo* (1966; London and New York: Routledge, 2001).

Dowling, Linda. "The Decadent and the New Woman in the 1890's," *Nineteenth-Century Fiction* 33, no. 4 (March 1979): 434–53.

Dowling, Linda. *Language and Decadence in the Victorian Fin de Siècle* (Princeton, NJ: Princeton University Press, 1986).

Doyle, Jennifer. "The Effects of Intimacy: Tracey Emin's Bad-Sex Aesthetics," in Mandy Merck and Chris Townsend (eds), *The Art of Tracey Emin* (London: Thames & Hudson, 2002), 102–18.

Driscoll, Lawrence. *Reconsidering Drugs: Mapping Victorian and Modern Drug Discourses* (New York: Palgrave, 2000).

Drouin-Brisebois, Josée (ed.). "Ornamental Impulse," in *Otherworld Uprising* (Montreal: Conundrum Press, 2008), 27–39.

D'Souza, Aruna and Tom McDonough (eds). *The Invisible* Flâneuse?: *Gender, Public Space and Visual Culture in Nineteenth-Century Paris* (Manchester and New York: Manchester University Press, 2006).

Duncan, Carol. "The MoMA's Hot Mamas," in *The Aesthetics of Power: Essays in Critical Art History* (Cambridge: Cambridge University Press, 1993), 189–207.

Duncan, Carol. "Virility and Domination in Early Twentieth-Century Vanguard Painting," in *The Aesthetics of Power: Essays in Critical Art History* (Cambridge: Cambridge University Press, 1993), 81–108.

Dyer, Richard. *White: Essays on Race and Culture* (London and New York: Routledge, 1997).

Eccher, Danilo, (ed.). "Ghada Amer," in *Ghada Amer* (Rome: Museo d'Arte Contemporanea Roma, 2007), 92–112.

Echols, Alice. *Daring to Be Bad: Radical Feminism in America 1967-1975* (Minneapolis: University of Minnesota Press, 1989).

Edmondson, Belinda. "Black Aesthetics, Feminist Aesthetics, and the Problems of Oppositional Discourse," in Hilary Robinson (ed.), *Feminist/Art/Theory: An Anthology 1968-2000* (Massachusetts: Blackwell Publishing, 2001), 325–41.

Elliott, Bridget. "Housing the Work: Women Artists, Modernism and the *maison d'artiste*: Eileen Gray, Romaine Brooks and Gluck," in Bridget Elliott and Janice Helland (eds), *Women Artists and the Decorative Arts 1880-1935: The Gender of Ornament* (Aldershot, UK and Burlington, VT: Ashgate, 2002), 176–91.

Elliott, Bridget. "Performing the Picture or Painting the Other: Romaine Brooks, Gluck and the Question of Decadence in 1923," in Katy Deepwell (ed.), *Women Artists and Modernism* (Manchester and New York: Manchester University Press, 1998), 70–82.

Elliott, Bridget and Janice Helland. "Introduction," in Bridget Elliott and Janice Helland (eds), *Women Artists and the Decorative Arts, 1880-1935: The Gender of Ornament* (Aldershot, UK and Burlington, VT: Ashgate, 2002), 1–14.

Elliott, Patrick (ed.). "Becoming Tracey Emin," in *Tracey Emin 20 Years* (Edinburgh: National Galleries of Scotland, 2008), 17–33.

Ettorre, Elizabeth. *Revisioning Women and Drug Use: Gender, Power and the Body* (New York: Palgrave Macmillan, 2007).

Felski, Rita. *The Gender of Modernity* (Cambridge, MA and London: Harvard University Press, 1995).

Fennetaux, Arianne. "Fashioning Death/Gendering Sentiment: Mourning Jewelry in Britain in the Eighteenth Century," in Maureen Daly Goggin and Beth Fowkes Tobin (eds), *Women and the Material Culture of Death* (Farnham, UK and Burlington, VT: Ashgate, 2013), 27–50.

Foster, Hal. "The Art of Fetishism: Notes on Dutch Still Life," in Emily Apter and William Pketz (eds), *Fetishism as Cultural Discourse* (Ithaca and London: Cornell University Press, 1993), 251–65.

Friedman, Jennifer and Marisa Alicea. "Women and Heroin: The Path of Resistance and its Consequences," *Gender and Society* 9, no. 4 (August 1995): 432–49.

Frueh, Joanna. "Making a Mess: Women's Bane, Women's Pleasure," in Katy Deepwell (ed.), *Women Artists and Modernism* (Manchester and New York: Manchester University Press, 1998), 142–58.

Gamman, Lorraine and Merja Makinen. *Female Fetishism: A New Look* (London: Lawrence & Wishart, 1994).

Garnet, Carla (ed.). "Allyson Mitchell: The Ladies Sasquatch, Theory and Practice," in *Allyson Mitchell: Ladies Sasquatch* (Hamilton, ON: The McMaster Museum of Art, 2009), 14–19.

Gouma-Peterson, Thalia. "Faith Ringgold's Journey: From Greek Busts to African Dilemma Tales," in Dan Cameron (ed.), *Faith Ringgold's French Collection and Other Story Quilts* (New York: New Museum of Contemporary Art, 1998), 39–48.

Gilman, Richard. *Decadence: The Strange Life of an Epithet* (New York: Farrar, Straus and Giroux, 1975).

Gilman, Sander. "The Hottentot and the Prostitute: Toward an Iconography of Female Sexuality," in Kymberly N. Pinder (ed.), *Race-ing Art History: Critical Readings in Race and Art History* (New York and London: Routledge, 2002), 119–38.

Gimpel, Jean. *Against Art and Artists* (1968; Edinburgh: Polygon, 1991).

Goggin, Maureen Daly. "Stitching (in) Death: Eighteenth- and Nineteenth-Century American and English Mourning Samplers," in Maureen Daly Goggin and Beth Fowkes Tobin (eds), *Women and the Material Culture of Death* (Farnham, UK and Burlington, VT: Ashgate, 2013), 63–89.

Goggin, Maureen Daly and Beth Fowkes Tobin (eds). *Women and the Material Culture of Needlework and Textiles, 1750-1950* (Farnham, UK and Burlington, VT: Ashgate, 2009).

Green, Martin. *Children of the Sun: A Narrative of "Decadence" in England After 1918* (New York: Basic Books, 1976).

Gunzburger Anderson, Cecilia. "We Are What We Wear: Cross-Cultural Uses of Textiles," in Ellen
    Rudolph (ed.), *Pattern ID* (Akron, OH: Akron Art Museum, 2010), 69–75.
Halberstam, Judith. *The Queer Art of Failure* (Durham, NC and London: Duke University Press,
    2011).
Hamlyn, Anne. "Freud, Fabric, Fetish," *Textile: The Journal of Cloth and Culture* 1, no. 1
    (2003): 9–27.
Hamlyn, Anne. "Freud, Fabric, Fetish," in Jessica Hemmings (ed.), *The Textile Reader* (London and
    New York: Berg, 2012), 14–26.
Hatt, Michael. "Space, Surface, Self: Homosexuality and the Aesthetic Interior," *Visual Culture in
    Britain* 8, no. 1 (Summer 2007): 105–28.
Helland, Janice. *British and Irish Home Arts and Industries, 1880-1914: Marketing Craft, Making
    Fashion* (Dublin and Portland, OR: Irish Academic Press, 2007).
Helland, Janice. *Professional Women Painters in Nineteenth-Century Scotland: Commitment,
    Friendship, Pleasure* (Aldershot, UK and Brookfield, VT: Ashgate, 2000).
Helland, Janice. *The Studios of Frances and Margaret MacDonald* (New York: St Martin's Press,
    1996).
Hemmings, Clare. *Why Stories Matter: The Political Grammar of Feminist Theory* (Durham, NC
    and London: Duke University Press, 2011).
Hemmings, Jessica (ed.). *The Textile Reader* (London and New York: Berg, 2012).
Hickman, Timothy A. "Heroin Chic: The Visual Culture of Narcotic Addiction," *Third Text* 16, no. 2
    (2002): 119–36.
Holt, Emily. "Flour Girls," *Vogue* (October 2013): 224–28.
hooks, bell. *Black Looks: Race and Representation* (Toronto: Between the Lines, 1992).
hooks, bell. "Aesthetic Inheritances: History Worked by Hand," in Joan Livingstone and John Ploof
    (eds), *The Object of Labour: Art, Cloth, and Cultural Production* (Chicago: School of the Art
    Institute of Chicago Press, 2007), 326–32.
Hopkins, David. "'Out of It': Drunkenness and Ethics in Martha Rosler and Gillian Wearing," in
    Gill Perry (ed.), *Difference and Excess in Contemporary Art: The Visibility of Women's Practice*
    (Malden, MA and Oxford: Blackwell Publishing, 2004), 22–45.
Hughes, Philip. "Preface," in Mary Schoeser, *Rozanne Hawksley* (North Wales and Farnham, UK/
    Burlington, VT: Ruthin Craft Centre and Lund Humphries, 2009), 9.
Huneault, Kristina. *Difficult Subjects: Working Women and Visual Culture, Britain 1880-1914*
    (Aldershot, UK and Burlington, VT: Ashgate, 2002).
Huneault, Kristina. "Professionalism as Critical Concept and Historical Process for Women and
    Art in Canada," in Kristina Huneault and Janice Anderson (eds), *Rethinking Professionalism:
    Women and Art in Canada, 1850-1970* (Montreal and Kingston: McGill-Queen's University
    Press, 2012), 3–52.
Hung, Shu and Joseph Magliaro (eds). *By Hand: The Use of Craft in Contemporary Art* (New York:
    Princeton Architectural Press, 2007).
I Want Candy: The Sweet Stuff in American Art (Yonkers, NY: Hudson River Museum, 2007).
Jacques, Michelle. "Art and History," in Louise Déry (ed.), *Shary Boyle: Flesh and Blood* (Montreal:
    Galerie l'UQAM, 2010), 129–37.
Jefferies, Janis. "Contemporary Textiles: The Art Fabric," in Nadine Monem (ed.), *Contemporary
    Textiles: The Fabric of Fine Art* (London: Black Dog Publishing, 2008), 36–61.
Jefferies, Janis. "Laboured Cloth: Translations of Hybridity in Contemporary Art," in Joan
    Livingstone and John Ploof (eds), *The Object of Labour: Art, Cloth, and Cultural Production*
    (Chicago: School of the Art Institute of Chicago Press, 2007), 284–94.
Jefferies, Janis. "Loving Attention: An Outburst of Craft in Contemporary Art," in Maria Elena
    Buszek (ed.), *Extra/Ordinary: Craft and Contemporary Art* (Durham, NC and London: Duke
    University Press, 2011), 222–40.
Jefferies, Janis. "Textiles," in Fiona Carson and Claire Pajaczkowska (eds), *Feminist Visual Culture*
    (New York and London: Routledge, 2001), 189–206.

Jefferies, Janis Diana Wood Conroy, and Hazel Clark (eds). *The Handbook of Textile Culture* (London: Bloomsbury, 2016).

Jones, Amelia. *Body Art/Performing the Subject* (Minneapolis: University of Minnesota Press, 1998).

Jullian, Philippe. *Dreamers of Decadence: Symbolist Painters of the 1890s*, trans. Robert Baldick (New York: Praeger Publishers, 1971).

Keane, Helen. *What's Wrong with Addiction?* (New York: New York University Press, 2002).

Kelley, Victoria. "The Interpretation of Surface: Boundaries, Systems and their Transgression in Clothing and Domestic Textiles, *c.* 1880-1939," *Textile: The Journal of Cloth & Culture* 7, no. 2 (July 2009): 216–35.

Kern, Leslie. *Sex and the Revitalized City: Gender, Condominium Development, and Urban Citizenship* (Vancouver and Toronto: University of British Columbia Press, 2010).

Kokoli, Alexandra M. "Introduction: Looking On, Bouncing Back," in Alexandra M. Kokoli (ed.), *Feminism Reframed* (Newcastle, UK: Cambridge Scholars Publishing, 2008), 1–18.

Kokoli, Alexandra M. "'Not a Straight Line but a Spiral': Charting Continuity and Change in Textiles Informed by Feminism," *Image & Text* 23 (2014): 110–29.

Kokoli, Alexandra M. "On Probation: 'Tracey Emin' as Sign," *Wasafiri* 25, no. 1 (2010): 33–40.

Kokoli, Alexandra M. "Sisters," in Rachel Dickson (ed.), *Judy Chicago and Louise Bourgeois, Helen Chadwick, Tracey Emin* (London: Lund Humphries, 2012), 169–77.

Kraft, Kerstin. "Textile Patterns and their Epistemological Function," *Textile: The Journal of Cloth and Craft* 3, no. 3 (Autumn 2004): 275–89.

Kriz, Kay Dian. *Slavery, Sugar, and the Culture of Refinement: Picturing the British West Indies, 1700-1840* (New Haven: Yale University Press, 2008).

Landers, Sean. "Mickalene Thomas," *Bomb* 116 (Summer 2011), http://bombmagazine.org/article/5105/mickalene-thomas (accessed July 2, 2015).

Lauzon, Claudette. "What the Body Remembers: Rebecca Belmore's Memorial to Missing Women," in Olivier Asselin, Johanne Lamoureux and Christine Ross (eds), *Precarious Visualities: New Perspectives on Identification in Contemporary* Art and *Visual Culture* (Montreal and Kingston: McGill-Queen's University Press, 2008), 155–79.

Livingstone, Joan and John Ploof (eds). *The Object of Labour: Art, Cloth, and Cultural Production* (Chicago: School of the Art Institute of Chicago Press, 2007).

Lucie-Smith, Edward. *Symbolist Art* (London: Thames and Hudson, 1993).

Mainardi, Patricia. "Quilts: The Great American Art," in Norma Broude and Mary D. Garrard (eds), *Feminism and Art History: Questioning the Litany* (New York: Harper & Row, 1982), 330–46.

Marcus, Jane. *Art and Anger: Reading Like a Woman* (Columbus: Ohio State University Press, 1988).

Mars, Tanya and Johanna Householder (eds). *Caught in the Act: An Anthology of Performance Art by Canadian Women* (Toronto: YYZ Books, 2004).

Mastai, Judith. "The Anorexic Body: Contemporary Installation Art by Women Artists in Canada," in Griselda Pollock (ed.), *Generations and Geographies in the Visual Arts: Feminist Readings* (London and New York: Routledge, 1996), 135–45.

McBrinn, Joseph. "'Male Trouble': Sewing, Amateurism, and Gender," in Elaine Cheasley Paterson and Susan Surette (eds), *Sloppy Craft: Postdisciplinarity and the Crafts* (London: Bloomsbury, 2015), 27–43.

McFadden, David Revere. *Radical Lace and Subversive Knitting* (New York: Museum of Arts and Design, 2007).

Menon, Elizabeth K. "Decadent Addictions: Tobacco, Alcohol, Popular Imagery, and Café Culture in France," in Laurinda S. Dixon (ed.), with the assistance of Gabriel P. Weisberg, *In Sickness and in Health: Disease as Metaphor in Art and Popular Wisdom* (Newark: University of Delaware Press, 2004), 101–24.

Mercer, Kobena. "Black Hair/Style Politics," in Russell Ferguson, Martha Gever, Trinh T. Min-ha, and Cornel West (eds), *Out There: Marginalization and Contemporary Cultures* (New York: The New Museum of Contemporary Art, 1990), 247–64.

Milligan, Barry. *Pleasures and Pains: Opium and the Orient in Nineteenth-Century British Culture* (Charlottesville and London: University Press of Virginia, 1995).

Mills, Josephine. "The Answer is Two Years Spent Baking Vulva-Shaped Cookies or, On Understanding Lesbian Representation," in Carla Garnet (ed.), *Allyson Mitchell: Ladies Sasquatch* (Hamilton, ON: The McMaster Museum of Art, 2009), 20–25.

Minor, Vernon Hyde. *Baroque Visual Rhetoric* (Toronto: University of Toronto Press, 2016).

Mitchell, Allyson (ed.). "A Call to Arms," in *When Women Rule the World: Judy Chicago in Thread* (Toronto: Textile Museum of Canada, 2009), 15–24.

Mitchell, Allyson. "Deep Lez I Statement," in Carla Garnet (ed.), *Allyson Mitchell: Ladies Sasquatch* (Hamilton, ON: The McMaster Museum of Art, 2009), 12–13.

Mitchell, Allyson (ed.). *Turbo Chicks: Talking Young Feminisms* (Toronto: Sumach Press, 2001).

Monem, Nadine. *Contemporary Textiles: The Fabric of Fine Art* (London: Black Dog Publishing, 2008).

Mosse, George L. "Masculinity and the Decadence," in Roy Porter and Mikuláš Teich (eds), *Sexual Knowledge, Sexual Science: The History of Attitudes to Sexuality* (Cambridge: Cambridge University Press, 1994), 251–66.

Muir, Gregor. *Lucky Kunst: The Rise and Fall of Young British Art* (London: Aurum Press, 2012).

Nead, Lynda. *Myths of Sexuality: Representations of Women in Victorian Britain* (Oxford: Basil Blackwell, 1990).

Nead, Lynda. *Victorian Babylon: People, Streets, and Images in Nineteenth-Century London* (New Haven and London: Yale University Press, 2000).

Nelson, Charmaine A. *The Color of Stone: Sculpting the Black Female Subject in Nineteenth-Century America* (Minneapolis and London: University of Minnesota Press, 2007).

Nelson, Charmaine A. *Representing the Black Female Subject in Western Art* (New York and London: Routledge, 2010).

Ngô, Fiona I. B. *Imperial Blues: Geographies of Race and Sex in Jazz Age New York* (Durham, NC and London: Duke University Press, 2014).

Nochlin, Linda. *Women, Art, and Power and Other Essays* (New York: Harper and Row, 1988).

Nordau, Max. *Degeneration* (1892; Lincoln and London: University of Nebraska Press, 2006).

O'Malley, Pat and Mariana Valverde. "Pleasure, Freedom and Drugs: The Uses of 'Pleasure' in Liberal Governance of Drug and Alcohol Consumption," *Sociology* 38, no. 1 (2004): 25–42.

Parker, Rozsika. *The Subversive Stitch: Embroidery and the Making of the Feminine* (1984; London and New York: I. B. Tauris, 2010).

Parker, Rozsika and Griselda Pollock. *Old Mistresses: Women, Art and Ideology* (London: Routledge and Kegan Paul, 1981).

Paterson, Elaine Cheasley and Susan Surette. "Introduction," in Elaine Cheasley Paterson and Susan Surette (eds), *Sloppy Craft: Postdisciplinarity and the Crafts* (London: Bloomsbury, 2015), 1–21.

Perry, Gill. "Introduction," in Gill Perry (ed.), *Difference and Excess in Contemporary Art: The Visibility of Women's Practice* (Oxford: Blackwell Publishing, 2004), 1–21.

Phelan, Peggy. *Unmarked: The Politics of Performance* (New York and London: Routledge, 1993).

Plant, Martin and Moira Plant. *Binge Britain: Alcohol and the National Response* (Oxford: Oxford University Press, 2006).

Pointon, Marcia. "Materializing Mourning: Hair, Jewellery and the Body," in Marius Kwint, Christopher Breward, and Jeremy Aynsley (eds), *Material Memories: Design and Evocation* (Oxford and New York: Berg, 1999), 39–57.

Pollock, Griselda, *Differencing the Canon: Feminist Desire and the Writing of Art's Histories* (New York and London: Routledge, 1999).

Pollock, Griselda, *Vision and Difference: Femininity, Feminism and Histories of Art* (New York and London: Routledge, 1988).

Pollock, Griselda. "What is it that Feminist Interventions Do?: Feminism and Difference in Retrospect and Prospect," in Alexandra M. Kokoli (ed.), *Feminism Reframed* (Newcastle, UK: Cambridge Scholars Publishing, 2008), 248–80.

Porter, David. "Monstrous Beauty: Eighteenth-Century Fashion and the Aesthetics of Chinese Taste," *Eighteenth-Century Studies* 35, no. 3 (2002): 395–411.

Potvin, John. "The Velvet Masquerade: Fashion, Interior Design and the Furnished Body," in Alla Myzelev and John Potvin (eds), *Fashion, Interior Design and the Contours of Modern Identity* (Farnham, UK and Burlington, VT: Ashgate, 2009), 1–17.

Pricked: Extreme Embroidery (New York: Museum of Arts and Design, 2007).

Quinn, Bradley. "Textiles at the Cutting Edge," in Nadine Monem (ed.), *Contemporary Textiles: The Fabric of Fine Art* (London: Black Dog Publishing, 2008), 10–32.

Quinton, Sarah (ed.). "Close to You," in *Close to You: Contemporary Textiles, Intimacy and Popular Culture* (Toronto: Textile Museum of Canada, 2007), 4–35.

Quinton, Sarah. "Threads and Needles," in Allyson Mitchell (ed.), *When Women Rule the World: Judy Chicago in Thread* (Toronto: Textile Museum of Canada, 2009), 41–46.

Race, Kane. *Pleasure Consuming Medicine: The Queer Politics of Drugs* (Durham, NC and London: Duke University Press, 2009).

Rault, Jasmine. *Eileen Gray and the Design of Sapphic Modernity: Staying In* (Farnham and Burlington: Ashgate, 2011).

Reeves, Jimmie L. and Richard Campbell. *Cracked Coverage: Television News, The Anti-Cocaine Crusade, and the Reagan Legacy* (Durham, NC and London: Duke University Press, 1994).

Reilly, Maura. "Writing the Body: The Art of Ghada Amer," in Maura Reilly (ed.), *Ghada Amer* (New York: Gregory R. Miller & Co., 2010), 6–49.

Reinarman, Craig. "Policing Pleasure: Food, Drugs, and the Politics of Ingestion," *Gastronomica: The Journal of Food and Culture* 7, no. 3 (Summer 2007): 53–61.

Ridge, George Ross. "The 'Femme Fatale' in French Decadence," *The French Review* 34, no. 4 (February 1961): 352–60.

Roberts, Mary Louise. *Disruptive Acts: The New Woman in Fin-de-Siècle France* (Chicago: University of Chicago Press, 2002).

Robertson, Kirsty. "Rebellious Doilies and Subversive Stitches: Writing a Craftivist History," in Maria Elena Buszek (ed.), *Extra/Ordinary: Craft and Contemporary Art* (Durham, NC and London: Duke University Press, 2011), 184–203.

Ross, Christine. *The Aesthetics of Disengagement: Contemporary Art and Depression* (Minneapolis and London: University of Minnesota Press, 2006).

Rowley, Sue. "Craft, Creativity and Critical Practice," in Sue Rowley (ed.), *Reinventing Textiles*, vol. 1: Tradition & Innovation (Winchester, UK: Telos, 1999), 1–20.

Rudolph, Ellen (ed.). "The Cultural Currency of Pattern and Dress," in *Pattern ID* (Akron, OH: Akron Art Museum, 2010), 11–23.

Russo, Mary. *The Female Grotesque: Risk, Excess and Modernity* (New York and London: Routledge, 1994).

Schaffer, Talia and Kathy Alexis Psomiades. "Introduction," in Talia Schaffer and Kathy Alexis Psomiades (eds), *Women and British Aestheticism* (Charlottesville and London: University of Virginia Press, 1999), 1–22.

Schnabel, Julian. "The Loneliness of the Long-Distance Runner," in Patrick Elliott (ed.), *Tracey Emin 20 Years* (Edinburgh: National Galleries of Scotland, 2008), 11–15.

Schoeser, Mary. *More is More: An Antidote to Minimalism* (London: Conran Octopus, 2001).

Schoeser, Mary. *Rozanne Hawksley* (North Wales and Farnham, UK/Burlington, VT: Ruthin Craft Centre and Lund Humphries, 2009).

Schor, Naomi. *Reading in Detail: Aesthetics and the Feminine* (1987; New York and London: Routledge, 2007).

Sedgwick, Eve Kosofsky. "Epidemics of the Will," in *Tendencies* (Durham, NC and London: Duke University Press, 1993), 13–42.

Showalter, Elaine. *The Female Malady: Women, Madness, and English Culture, 1830-1980* (New York: Penguin Books, 1985).

Showalter, Elaine. "Introduction," in Elaine Showalter (ed.), *Daughters of Decadence: Women Writers of the Fin-de-Siècle* (London: Virago, 1993), vii–xx.

Showalter, Elaine. *Sexual Anarchy: Gender and Culture at the Fin de Siècle* (London: Bloomsbury, 1991).

Siegel, Jonah. *Desire and Excess: The Nineteenth-Century Culture of Art* (Princeton: Princeton University Press, 2000).

Siegel, Sandra. "Literature and Degeneration: The Representation of 'Decadence,'" in J. Edward Chamberlin and Sander L. Gilman (eds), *Degeneration: The Dark Side of Progress* (New York: Columbia University Press, 1985), 199–219.

Skelly, Julia. "Object Lessons: The Social Life of Temperance Banners," *Textile: The Journal of Cloth and Culture* 14, no. 3 (2016): 268–93.

Skelly, Julia. "The Paradox of Excess: Oscar Wilde, Caricature, and Consumption," in Julia Skelly (ed.), *The Uses of Excess in Visual* and *Material* Culture, *1600-2010* (Farnham, UK and Burlington, VT: Ashgate, 2014), 137–60.

Skelly, Julia (ed.). *The Uses of Excess in Visual and Material* Culture, *1600-2010* (Farnham, UK and Burlington, VT: Ashgate, 2014).

Skelly, Julia. *Wasted Looks: Addiction and British Visual Culture, 1751-1919* (Farnham, UK and Burlington, VT: Ashgate, 2014).

Sloboda, Stacey. *Chinoiserie: Commerce and Critical Ornament in Eighteenth-Century Britain* (Manchester and New York: Manchester University Press, 2014).

Sloboda, Stacey. "Porcelain Bodies: Gender, Acquisitiveness, and Taste in Eighteenth-Century England," in John Potvin and Alla Myzelev (eds), *Material Cultures, 1740-1920: The Meanings and Pleasures of Collecting* (Aldershot, UK and Burlington, VT: Ashgate, 2009), 19–36.

Smith, Sarah E. K. "Bringing Queer Theory into Queer Practice," in Sarah E. K. Smith (ed.), *I'm Not Myself At All* (Kingston, ON: Agnes Etherington Art Centre, 2015), 22–31.

Smith, T'ai. *Bauhaus Weaving Theory: From Feminine Craft to Mode of Design* (Minneapolis and London: University of Minnesota Press, 2014).

Solnit, Rebecca. *Men Explain Things to Me* (Chicago: Haymarket Books, 2014).

Sorkin, Jenni. "Stain: On Cloth, Stigma, and Shame," *Third Text* 14, no. 53 (2000): 77–80.

Sorkin, Jenni. "Stain: On Cloth, Stigma, and Shame," in Jessica Hemmings (ed.), *The Textile Reader* (London and New York: Berg, 2012), 59–63.

Stevens, Dennis. "Validity Is in the Eye of the Beholder: Mapping Craft Communities of Practice," in Maria Elena Buszek (ed.), *Extra/Ordinary: Craft and Contemporary Art* (Durham, NC and London: Duke University Press, 2011), 43–58.

St-Gelais, Thérèse. "The *Others* of Pleasure and Love," in Thérèse St-Gelais (ed.), *Ghada Amer* (Montreal: Musée d'art contemporain de Montréal, 2012), 64–79.

Suzuki, Jūzō and Isaburō Oka. *Masterworks of Ukiyo-E: "The Decadents"* trans. John Bester (Tokyo, Japan and Palo Alto, CA: Kodansha International Ltd., 1969).

Tanner, Marcia. "Mother Laughed: The Bad Girls' Avant-Garde," in Marcia Tanner and Marcia Tucker (eds), *Bad Girls*, exh. cat. (New York: The New Museum of Contemporary Art/Cambridge, MA: The MIT Press, 1994), 47–80.

Tanner, Marcia. "Preface," in Marcia Tanner and Marcia Tucker (eds), *Bad Girls*, exh. cat. (New York: The New Museum of Contemporary Art/Cambridge, MA: The MIT Press, 1994), 10–13.

Tanner, Marcia and Marcia Tucker. *Bad Girls*, exh. cat. (New York: The New Museum of Contemporary Art/Cambridge, MA: The MIT Press, 1994).

Temple, Ruth. "Truth in Labelling: Pre-Raphaelitism, Aestheticism, Decadence, Fin de Siècle," *ELT* 17 (1974): 201–22.

Terry, Charles E. and Mildred Pellens. *The Opium Problem* (New York: The Committee on Drug Addictions in Collaboration with the Bureau of Social Hygiene, 1928).

Tesfagiorgis, Freida High W. "Afrofemcentrism and its Fruition in the Art of Elizabeth Catlett and Faith Ringgold," in Norma Broude and Mary D. Garrard (eds), *The Expanding Discourse: Feminism and Art History* (New York: HarperCollins, 1992), 475–85.

Tickner, Lisa. "Banners and Banner-Making," in Vanessa R. Schwartz and Jeannene M. Przyblyski (eds), *The Nineteenth-Century Visual Culture Reader* (New York and London: Routledge, 2004), 341–48.

Tickner, Lisa. *The Spectacle of Women: Images of the Suffrage Campaign, 1907-14* (Chicago and London: University of Chicago Press, 1988).

Tobin, Beth Fowkes and Maureen Daly Goggin. "Connecting Women and Death: An Introduction," in Maureen Daly Goggin and Beth Fowkes Tobin (eds), *Women and the Material Culture of Death* (Farnham, UK and Burlington, VT: Ashgate, 2013), 1–17.

Traub, Valerie. *Desire and Anxiety: Circulations of Sexuality in Shakespearean Drama* (New York and London: Routledge, 1992).

Tucker, Marcia. "Introduction," in Marcia Tanner and Marcia Tucker (eds), *Bad Girls*, exh. cat. (New York: The New Museum of Contemporary Art/Cambridge, MA: The MIT Press, 1994), 4–9.

Vance, Carole S. (ed.). *Pleasure and Danger: Exploring Female Sexuality* (1984; London: Pandora Press, 1992).

Viano, Maurizio. "An Intoxicated Screen: Reflections on Film and Drugs," in Janet Farrell Brodie and Marc Redfield (eds), *High Anxieties: Cultural Studies in Addiction* (Berkeley: University of California Press, 2002), 134–58.

Vincentelli, Moira. *Women and Ceramics: Gendered Vessels* (Manchester and New York: Manchester University Press, 2000).

Wahl, Kimberly. *Dressed as in a Painting: Women and British Aestheticism in an Age of Reform* (Durham and New Hampshire: University of New Hampshire Press, 2013).

Wallace, Michele (ed.). *Faith Ringgold: Twenty Years of Painting, Sculpture and Performance (1963-1983)* (New York: Studio Museum in Harlem, 1984).

Wark, Jayne. *Radical Gestures: Feminism and Performance Art in North America* (Montreal and Kingston: McGill-Queen's University Press, 2006).

Weichel, Eric. "'Every Other Place it Could be Placed with Advantage': Ladies-in-Waiting at the British Court and the 'Excessive' Display of Ceramics as Art Objects, 1689-1740," in Julia Skelly (ed.), *The Uses of Excess in Visual and Material Culture, 1600-2010* (Farnham, UK and Burlington, VT: Ashgate, 2014), 41–61.

Weir, David. *Decadence and the Making of Modernism* (Amherst: University of Massachusetts Press, 1995).

"Who's Bad? A Mixed Response to a Season of Bad Girls," *Frieze*, issue 15 (March/April 1994) http://www.frieze.com/issue/article/whos_bad/ (accessed December 15, 2015).

Wilde, Oscar, *The Picture of Dorian Gray* (1891; Hertfordshire: Wordsworth Editions Limited, 2001).

Wilson, Elizabeth. *The Sphinx in the City: Urban Life, the Control of Disorder, and Women* (London: Virago Press, 1991).

Wolff, Janet. "The Invisible *Flâneuse*: Women and the Literature of Modernity," in *Feminine Sentences: Essays on Women and Culture* (Berkeley and Los Angeles: University of California Press, 1990), 34–50.

Wood, Marcus. "John Gabriel Stedman, William Blake, Francesco Bartolozzi and Empathetic Pornography in the *Narrative of a Five Years Expedition against the Revolted Negroes of Surinam*," in Geoff Quilley and Kay Dian Kriz (eds), *An Economy of Colour: Visual Culture and the Atlantic World, 1660-1830* (Manchester and New York: Manchester University Press, 2003), 129–49.

Woodman, Marion. *Addiction to Perfection: The Still Unravished Bride* (Toronto: Inner City Books, 1982).

Yardley, Tom. *Why We Take Drugs: Seeking Excess and Communion in the Modern World* (New York and London: Routledge, 2012).

Zambreno, Kate. *Heroines* (Los Angeles: Semiotext(e), 2012).

Zatlin, Linda Gertner. *Beardsley, Japonisme, and the Perversion of the Victorian Ideal* (Cambridge: Cambridge University Press, 1997).

Zieger, Susan. "'How Far am I Responsible?': Women and Morphinomania in Late-Nineteenth-Century Britain," *Victorian Studies* 48, no. 1 (Autumn 2005): 59–81.

INDEX

INDEX   **125**